"The Merlot would pair better. Its notes complement the dish."

"The loose brush strokes are what make this a truly classic work of Impressionist art."

"I haven't seen a witch hunt like this since McCarthy's HUAC hearings."

"When it comes to geological time periods, I've always been quite partial to the Phanerozoic Eon, myself."

"That's so interesting. I've always found the Russian Split Jump to be one of the more impressive moves in figure skating."

"What a coincidence! I can't believe someone else here likes German Expressionist architecture as much as I do!"

"I definitely saw that ending coming. It's a post-modern work after all."

"It's a no-brainer. The potential ROI will outweigh the start-up costs."

"Have I read it? I don't think there's a Post-Victorian Gothic book I haven't read."

"It's simple really. It's just an exercise in supply-side economics."

"The Merlot would pair better. Its berry notes complement the dish."

Fake It 'til You Make It *in Work, Love, and Life*

THE
Bullsh*t
Artist

Learn to **Bluff, Dupe, Charm,** and **BS** with the Best of 'Em

"I definitely saw that ending coming. It's a post-modern work after all."

"It's a no-brainer. The potential ROI will outweigh the start-up costs."

PAUL KLEINMAN

"It's simple really. It's just an exercise in supply-side economics."

Aadamsmedia
Avon, Massachusetts

Published by
Adams Media, a division of F+W Media, Inc.
57 Littlefield Street, Avon, MA 02322. U.S.A.
www.adamsmedia.com

ISBN 10: 1-4405-1255-8
ISBN 13: 978-1-4405-1255-1
eISBN 10: 1-4405-2724-5
eISBN 13: 978-1-4405-2724-1

Printed in the United States of America.

10   9   8   7   6   5   4   3   2   1

Library of Congress Cataloging-in-Publication Data
Kleinman, Paul.
The bullsh*t artist / Paul Kleinman.
p. cm.
Includes bibliographical references.
ISBN 978-1-4405-1255-1
1. Conduct of life—Humor. I. Title.
PN6231.C6142K56 2011
818'.602—dc22
2011010390

certificate illustration © iStockphoto.com / kirstypargeter

This book is available at quantity discounts for bulk purchases.
For information, please call 1-800-289-0963.

This book is dedicated to the memory of my father.

ACKNOWLEDGMENTS

My deepest gratitude to my family and Lizzie. Thank you for all of your support and for putting up with my bullshit for so long. It looks like it's finally paid off.

Contents

Introduction

When it comes to information, there is a lot to take in. In a world dominated by twenty-four-hour-news channels (bullshit), pornography (bullshit), and Miley Cyrus (~~bullshit~~ voice of an angel), information practically suffocates us at all times of the day. It's impossible to know everything on any given subject. But frankly, it's not about what you know, but what you don't know. And more importantly, how you react in circumstances when you *need* to know what you *don't* know. You don't have to throw in the towel once you feel you don't have anything to contribute to the conversation. What you do is bullshit.

And it's not as simple as it sounds.

Good bullshit is like a fine wine. As it matures, it gets better. It shouldn't stay bottled up forever and it shouldn't come spilling out. After the right amount of time, the perfect amount should be poured and sipped casually. And like any good art, bullshit takes practice to get perfect. This book should serve as a mentor so that you too can become a Bullshit Artist.

Let's say you're meeting your girlfriend or boyfriend's father for the first time and you want to make a good first impression. It turns out he's a World War II buff and history wasn't exactly your strong suit growing up. You might have difficulty holding a conversation with him—unless of course, you can think on your feet.

Or maybe you've finally summoned enough courage to talk to that hot girl across the bar and it turns out she's completing a master's in philosophy and has a soft spot for David Hume. Guessing you don't have a clue who the guy is, but you don't necessarily have to know about Hume to make her *think* you do.

The thing is, if you want to be successful in this world, you don't actually have to walk the walk, but you've definitely got to talk the talk. And in order to do so, it's going to take some training. We're talking mental training here,

Rocky, so put down the jump rope and Icy Hot. You can't be expected to know everything, but you can certainly fake it so people think otherwise.

So consider this your new Bible. Study it, learn it, and master it. This book will teach you everything you need to know in order to bullshit like the best of them. You'll get a rundown of various bullshitting techniques, along with helpful tips and pointers that just might save your ass one day.

But enough with the introductions—let's get started. You know, I'm sensing a little tremble in your hand. Maybe you should keep the Icy Hot out just in case.

"Her poetry practically brings me to tears."

"Trust me, as long as you diversify your investments, you'll be fine."

"The loose brush strokes are what make this a truly classic work of Impressionist art."

PART 1

The Art of Bullshitting

"Oh my God, I love country music too!"

"Have I read it? I don't think there's a Post-Victorian Gothic book I haven't read."

"I couldn't agree with you more. The true question is whether the Electoral College is even needed at all at this point."

"That's so interesting. I've always found the Russian Split Jump to be one of the more impressive moves in figure skating."

Chapter 1

On the Origin of Bullshit

"Bullshit is truly the American soundtrack."
—GEORGE CARLIN

Bullshit can be tricky. You can break bullshit down into two different types: Successful Bullshit and Spewed Shit. There's a fine line between bullshitting and just spewing shit and you need to know the differences between the two so you can pull off the former and avoid the latter.

What the Hell Is Successful Bullshit?

Successful Bullshit is the process of talking insincerely on something about which you honestly have no idea. A misrepresentation? Sure. Effective? Definitely.

Let's take a look at an example.

Eric sees a smoking-hot brunette across the café. He is instantly smitten and decides he has to make his move. As he approaches, he notices she is reading a Nicholas Sparks novel. Eric sees his chance. Although he's never read a page of *The Notebook* or any of Sparks's other books, he's heard of the guy, and if he plays his cards right, they could potentially spend some "nights in Rodanthe" together.

Eric pretends to bump into the reader, named Lindsay, by accident. Executed perfectly. He apologizes, and as he does, he can't help but notice she is reading his "favorite" Nicholas Sparks book. What a coincidence, huh? Eric talks to her about how poetic Nicholas Sparks's writing is, and how last winter he curled up next to a fireplace and read that book in its entirety in one sitting. And yes, he admits, he shed a tear or two. He asks her, "Where are you in the book?" And when she tells him, he says, "Oh, I love that part. But I won't give anything away. It's too good."

A few hours pass and Sparks hasn't been mentioned since the initial encounter. The two exchange information and plan to meet up later that night. Eric succeeds in winning the girl. And it's all thanks to Nicholas Spar—bullshit. It's all thanks to bullshit.

You see, with Successful Bullshit, even if you have little or no foundation to work from, you speak as if you do. And here's the important part about Successful Bullshit: done right, it works. It really works. You get away with it. And best of all—you come out looking like an expert.

> Before we go any further, a warning is in order: bullshit is a lot like fire. Fire can do amazing things. It can keep you warm, cook your food, help you create tools, and even transform into energy. But fire can also be very dangerous. It can burn you, destroy your home, and melt your Rod Stewart collection (sorry, Dad). You've got to learn how to use fire to your advantage and keep it at bay. Bullshit is no different. You have to be in control of your bullshit and not let your bullshit control you.

Spewed Shit

To put it simply, Spewed Shit, or failed bullshit, is nonsense. It can be an obvious lie you get called out on, or it can be bizarre rambling that leaves others speechless (and not in a good way). This might sound complicated, but it isn't. Think about all the times you've said something, your friend replied, and you've yelled back to him, "Bullshit!" This is failed bullshit. He wasn't bullshitting. He was spewing shit. And there's a big difference.

HISTORICAL MOMENT OF SPEWED SHIT

JANUARY 26, 1998, PRESIDENT BILL CLINTON

WHAT HE SAID: "I did not have sexual relations with that woman, Miss Lewinsky."

WHAT HE WAS THINKING: *Except for those nine debriefings.*

How to Avoid Spewing Shit

You don't want to weave a web so thick that you get caught in it. You never want someone to know that you're bullshitting them. Return to the idea of fire for a moment: think of the pyromaniacs. They do stupid things like turn forests into giant balls of flame and videotape themselves in the act. Don't videotape your bullshit in the woods. Don't do things to get yourself caught. If you're caught, you've failed.

Steer clear of this failed bullshit in every way. This book isn't a guide to help you sound like a jackass. It's meant to help you succeed. You need to use your bullshitting powers for good, to help better yourself, and to get ahead.

To further understand just how detrimental spewing shit really is, check out this classic.

The Boy Who Cried Bull—a Lesson in Spewing Shit

Colin is a manly man. Correction. Colin wants people to *think* he is a manly man. No matter where Colin goes, if women are around, he has his go-to story. Colin's bullshit takes him back to the "good old days" where he was a star football player for the State University. Of course, Colin never played any football for any university and barely graduated from college, but what woman at this bar is going to know that?

He finds his target. She must be from out of town because he's never seen her before and he's somewhat of a regular around here. Within seconds, he approaches her and starts on about his days at State and how much he misses the game. Yep, he fancies himself something of a celebrity around these parts. It's all standard Colin (or so everyone inside the bar seems to be saying to each other in between bouts of laughter). Colin barely even looks up from the floor as he recites his tale practically from memory.

Not surprisingly, the woman doesn't show much interest in what he has to say, but hey, Colin keeps offering to buy drinks, so she'll put up with it a little longer. As he blabbers on, she whips out her phone and texts her friends.

Eventually, the drinks don't seem worth it anymore, and she asks her friends to come over and save her.

Her friends soon join in the conversation and they start asking Colin questions about his playing days. Colin seems to stumble over every answer and can't quite make a coherent sentence. The questions keep coming and Colin is far too deep into his bullshit to turn back now. He doesn't want to look like a loser in front of this girl or her friends, so he continues trying to answer in between the frequent "Ums" and "Well, uh, let me thinks." Soon, Colin notices lights all around him.

As Colin looks to his left and to his right, he sees phones of all shapes and sizes illuminating the women's faces. The women type away until suddenly one phone shines on Colin's face. The woman he is trying to entice holds her phone in front of Colin and asks, "If you played, how come I can't find information on you anywhere online?"

Colin opens his mouth, but words won't come out. His eyes quickly dart around the room and he appears visibly nervous. The questions continue. "What game did you say you scored that winning touchdown?" "Where were you playing?" "Who did you pass the ball to?" By the time he's able to think of something, the women are gone. Colin's bullshit has left him with sweat on his face and a hefty bar tab. As he looks around, he sees everyone else at the bar laughing and lots of eyes rolling. This indeed was standard Colin—and a perfect example of failed BS.

At some point, things can start getting a bit tricky. You see, sometimes seemingly Successful Bullshit can actually devolve into Spewed Shit. You want to make the other person eat out of the palm of your hands. But if you go overboard with your bullshit, they'll start to suspect something is up. Even worse, you might start to lose control of your own BS and not be able to backtrack. Think back to Colin. He dug himself into a hole so deep he couldn't climb out, even if someone handed him a ladder. His bullshit took on a life of its own and he lost control.

Remember: a successful bullshitter never loses control of his bullshit.

Your bullshit is like a game of chess. You've got to be strategic about where and how you place your pieces. Train yourself and focus on being smart with your bullshit. Don't be foolish or sound like an imbecile or it will be check and mate.

While examples abound in history of unsuccessful bullshitters, it proves much more difficult to uncover examples of raw bullshit ability. This is because real bullshitters don't get caught. They never let you know they are bullshitting you. After all, if you get caught, you're just a liar. A person has to be a true master in the art of bullshitting to be able to get away with it successfully.

Successful Bullshitter: Frank Abagnale, Jr.

Most of you probably know of Frank Abagnale, Jr., the real-life character Leonardo DiCaprio played in the film *Catch Me If You Can*. This impostor and con artist managed to pass $2.5 million worth of forged checks in twenty-six countries and take on eight separate identities including airline pilot, doctor, and lawyer. After he finally was caught, he was released fewer than five years into his prison sentence and went to work for the very people who put him in jail. Later, he became a security consultant and founded Abagnale & Associates. Today, Frank Abagnale, Jr., is a legitimate millionaire and helps stop the same kind of fraud he used to commit. As if that weren't enough, the film of his life story was the eleventh-highest grossing film of 2002. Not too bad for a bullshitter.

Shit Spewer: James Frey

In 2003, James Frey's book, *A Million Little Pieces*, hit the shelves. The book, a memoir about the author's personal struggle with his addiction to drugs and alcohol addiction and the rocky road to recovery, made the cut for the Oprah Book Club in 2005. Soon, it was at the top of the bestselling charts, number one on Amazon.com, and sold more than 3.5 million copies. Following Frey's appearance on Oprah during which he discussed his book (and subsequently made the Queen of Talk teary-eyed), the website *www.thesmokinggun.com* started an investigation on the "facts" found in the memoir.

Frey's lies began to unravel when folks discovered that much of the book had been embellished or fabricated. Among other things, Frey claimed to be inside of a train during an accident that left two women dead and claimed to have spent 83 days in jail when in reality he only spent a few hours in prison. The next time Frey appeared on *Oprah*, she was much less amicable and the author admitted to his lies. James Frey broke the number one rule of bullshitting: Never make your bullshit so extravagant that it sounds too good to be true. But maybe more importantly, never—and I mean *never*—bullshit Oprah.

Pop Quiz!

Don't you hate how textbooks have questions at the end of each chapter? It seems so demoralizing. It's almost as if to say the author has such a lack of faith in the reader's ability to comprehend things that he needs to trick the reader to see if he or she was actually paying attention. Now then, let's take a look at a sample question to see what you've learned so far.

SAMPLE QUESTION:

Monty graduated at the top of his class from Harvard Business School. Today, he has a job interview with a major corporation. Monty really wants this job. He sits in the waiting room until finally he hears his name. The receptionist tells him someone will be in shortly and to take a seat inside the office. As he sits, he notices something on the interviewer's desk. It's a playbill from the show *Wicked*. Monty hasn't seen *Wicked*, and frankly, doesn't think too highly of musical theater as a whole.

Now what, in this situation, would be considered Successful Bullshit?

A. This question.
B. Monty's ignoring the playbill on the desk, and going right into a discussion of his resume.
C. Monty's mentioning notice of the playbill, and telling the interviewer he never cared much for musicals.
D. Monty's mentioning notice of the playbill, and then telling the interviewer, "I've heard great things about *Wicked*. Did you enjoy it?"

The correct answer is D. Despite Monty's distaste for musical theater, he feigns an interest in order to set a friendly and engaging tone, thereby starting his interview on a much higher note (no pun intended).

Now what about those times when there isn't a playbill right in front of you? What about those times when you need to pull something out of thin air? The second half of this book provides you with quick and easy references for situations where you'd otherwise be clueless. That way, all you'll need to do is throw in a sentence here and there, and let the other person do the talking. You'll get enough information to seem like you know what you're talking about—and the others will be none the wiser.

QUESTIONS TO ASK YOURSELF:
- What is Successful Bullshit?
- What is Spewed Shit?
- Can you think of a successful bullshitter that you know? What does he/she do well?
- Can you think of a failed bullshitter? What went wrong?
- Why the hell was *Cats* so successful?

Good bullshit is all about survival of the fittest. Over time, if you use the right tools and train yourself, your bullshitting capabilities will evolve. And I'm not bullshitting you.

Chapter 2

Why Bullshitting Works

"Honesty is for the most part less profitable than dishonesty."

—PLATO

"We want people who hate to lose, like myself. Now marinate on that."

—SNOOP DOGG

If you've picked up this book, you probably already know bullshitting works. But why does it work? Why does bullshit, if done correctly, help you succeed?

The answer is simple. Bullshitting works because it lets you get away with your lies. Operating under false pretenses opens the door to conversations you never before would have thought possible. The truth is frequently a dead end. However, if you can manage to manipulate the truth to your advantage, the world is an open road and you're at the steering wheel. Buckle up, because from here, the possibilities for success are limitless.

Success is a powerful motivator. It can take many forms—financial, creative, romantic, or personal success—and the list can go on and on. To be a true Bullshit Artist, you must have an inner drive to succeed. Take a look at the quotes at the beginning of this chapter. Plato really taps into the reason bullshitting works so well. "Profitable" here does not necessarily have to be monetary—it can take any form you desire. And if one of the greatest thinkers of mankind is saying dishonesty is profitable, you'd better listen.

Mr. Dogg's take on success is also full of insight. Successful people hardly ever lose, and when they do, they know how to use it to their advantage. They are winners by definition and that's exactly what you want to be. To be a successful bullshitter, losing can't be an option. You should want to be successful and you should want to win. You should hate losing, and if you're caught in your bullshit, losing is exactly what you'll be doing. So please, do as the man says and marinate on that. It's what's best for you.

Here's another way to think about why bullshitting works: You start out at point A and need to get to point B as quickly and efficiently as possible so you decide to take a shortcut. Successful Bullshit is the shortcut.

Here's the breakdown:

Point A = Your starting point
Point B = Your goal or some sort of success (i.e., the desired end result)
Point A to Point B = The distance you must cover to achieve your goal
Bullshit = The shortcut

Bullshit is a tool that shortens your path to success by cutting down on your travel time. It is the way you can arrive at Point B faster without having to get caught up or bogged down with everything you would normally have to do (or learn, or know).

In most cases, you can see true success. When you were in school, you got gold stars and letter grades that showed your progress (=visible proof). A baseball pitcher reveals his ability by firing a ball at 100 miles per hour into the pitcher's glove (=visible proof). Good actors can really convince you they are the person they are portraying (=visible proof). A great architect's creation leaves you speechless as you stand before it (=visible proof).

Bullshit is different. There is no round of applause, no A+, no points on a scoreboard. If you're looking for kudos and a pat on the back for your excellent bullshit, sorry pal, but you're shit out of luck.

There are no bragging rights. You see, your Successful Bullshit has to be internalized. Otherwise you've let everyone in on the hoax, turning all of your hard work into Spewed Shit. That's not something a Bullshit Artist can afford.

This is not to say successful bullshitters don't have anything to show for their hard work. On the contrary, successful bullshitters have everything to show for their efforts. They have reached the goal they set out to accomplish, just without the "Good jobs" or "Atta boys." If you really need acknowledgment, pat yourself on the back when no one is around. Other than that, keep it to yourself.

Now, you might find this a little surprising, but your bullshit is only as good as you make it. The good news? If you continue training, your BS can always improve. In the next chapter, you'll get tips and exercises to help you hone your skills. Before we go there, you've got to know what it takes to be a successful bullshitter.

THE CHARACTERISTICS: A SUCCESSFUL BULLSHITTER IS:

1. Imaginative
2. Ballsy
3. Calm
4. Sly
5. Articulate
6. Confident
7. Charming
8. Attentive
9. Dishonest
10. Cautious

To better understand these qualities, first take a look at the following example.

David Versus the Goliath Assignment

David has to give a presentation to his boss in four hours. He was going to start preparing for it when it was assigned weeks ago, but he got too swept up in his fantasy football team . . . and reading about how to play guitar . . . and learning Spanish . . . and then there was that *My Super Sweet 16* marathon.

David should be feeling pretty screwed right now, but he's as cool as a cucumber. He shows up at his boss's office, and is greeted with the usual, "Ah, David. How is my star performer today?" In a corporation of 200 employees, David has made a name for himself. He has sat in on numerous presentations and meetings, participating frequently. David discovered early on that if he spoke up enough, not only would he not have to work as hard, but he'd get the attention of the higher-ups (and get them to *think* he was working hard).

David isn't his same old chatty self in this meeting, however, and his boss asks if everything is all right. That's when David goes in for the kill. He tells his boss about a dilemma he's been having with the presentation. Even though he started it weeks ago, David explains, he keeps changing his mind on how to approach it. He brings up some ideas (the few he paid attention to), and then says how he just doesn't think his presentation is reflective of his capabilities or the quality of work he's produced all year.

He tells his boss it's been worrying him to the point that he has actually been missing sleep for the past week and feels exhausted both mentally and physically. David appears nervous, but he is very clear and precise when he speaks to his boss. David sees concern in his boss's face, and then does something unexpected. David stands up, thanks him for his time, and begins to leave.

As he starts for the door, his boss stops him. "Hey, David." David turns around slowly. Here it comes. "Why don't you take a few days and hand it to me when you're ready?" David acts surprised by this. "No, I couldn't. That wouldn't be right." But his boss insists. When David leaves the office that day, he closes his briefcase with a big smile on his face. Mission accomplished.

At work the next day, as coworkers around David complain about how difficult their presentations were to write, David pretends he is in the same boat. He asks several colleagues what they wrote about, and they tell him, believing he is commiserating with them. Of course, David is not miserable at all. And now he has some ideas about how to craft his own report.

How did David get away with this? By employing the characteristics of a Successful Bullshitter. Let's break it down.

I. David Was Imaginative

Imagination is key to any true Bullshit Artist. It's hard to BS someone when you can't think of anything to say. When David approaches his boss, he has a sob story in hand. He doesn't go in there begging and pleading for an extension on the presentation, and he doesn't make mention of not starting it. Instead, he fabricates a lie.

You can go into a situation with a story already planned in its entirety, or partially, or you can make it up on the fly. If you do prepare a story, don't make it so concrete that it can't change. If someone throws a curve ball at you, be ready to swing the bat (and not strike out).

Also remember, don't go overboard with your creativity. Keep your story believable. Make it too imaginative, and you risk crossing into Spewed Shit territory. And once you're there, it's hard to get past border control.

HISTORICAL MOMENT OF SPEWED SHIT
1720—1797, FRIEDRICH VON MÜNCHHAUSEN
Friedrich von Münchhausen was perhaps one of the biggest shit spewers of all time. After returning home from war, Münchhausen began sharing stories of his adventures overseas. Naturally, these included going to the Moon, dancing in the stomach of a whale, and riding a cannon ball. Baron von Münchhausen is so well-known for his BS, two psychiatric disorders are named after him: Münchausen syndrome, in which a person feigns illness to get attention from doctors, and Münchausen syndrome by proxy, in which a person either lies to doctors that their child is sick, or actually makes their child sick in order to gain attention.

2. David Was Ballsy

David's got guts. In all fairness, after procrastinating on a major assignment, David should have to deal with the consequences like everyone else. Why should he be excused? What makes him special? Well, nothing makes him special—except his downright ballsiness and his mindset for bullshitting.

David takes the issue straight to the boss. He can't go any higher. If his boss sees through his lie, the situation can get much, much worse. Using bullshit as an aid, David sets out to achieve an almost impossible goal. This assignment was given weeks ago and he had plenty of time to get it done.

Why didn't he do it? He was lazy. Should he have to face the consequences? Absolutely. Will he? No chance.

You've got to be ballsy to be a successful Bullshit Artist. By misrepresenting yourself, you always risk someone's calling your bluff. How badly do you want something? How far are you willing to go to get it? You've got to put yourself out there if you want to succeed. There is no "playing it safe" when it comes to Successful Bullshit. You need to go out and make it happen.

Grab the bull by the balls and give it all you've got.

3. David Was Calm

David keeps his composure throughout. The ability to remain calm in a stressful situation is crucial if you want to succeed. You need to be able to compose yourself when the situation is otherwise chaotic or worrying. If you allow nerves to get the better of you, that nervousness can lead to mistakes. Impaired judgment and cluttered thought processes will rule. Make one too many mistakes and you may not be able to backpedal.

Mistakes doom a bullshitter. They are the tiny cracks in the dam that slowly leak—you know—Spewed Shit. If enough gets through the cracks, the whole wall can tumble down, and it can happen in a matter of seconds. You can't afford to make mistakes when bullshitting. You must keep your mind clutter free.

Now, I'm not telling you to be calm to the point of sedation. That won't help you either. Michael Caine put it best when he said, "Be like a duck. Calm on the surface, but always paddling like the dickens underneath." Your nerves should act as a series of checks and balances to your bullshit. Use them so you don't expose too much of your bullshit too quickly, but at the same time, don't let them take over and not let you get a word out.

Just take a breath when you start to feel anxious so you can work through the situation. You can sweat about it when you're alone. Right now, you've got some bullshitting to do.

4. David Was Sly

Now that your imagination is running wild, you've got the right amount of ballsiness to take on whatever comes your way, you have the ability to remain calm in the worst situations, and you are ready to begin the deception process. Remember when David started to head for his boss's door? This wasn't a sign of forfeit; it was a strategic move on David's part. At the very moment David could have asked for an extension, he didn't. Why wouldn't he ask? It's the only reason he's there, and he's just walking away. What gives?

The answer is simple: David knows how to play the game. By letting his boss bring up the extension, David doesn't come across as a whining student begging for help. The word "extension" never even crosses his lips. If something were to happen, his boss has no one else to blame but himself. After all, it was his idea to give the extension. At least, his boss *thinks* it was his idea.

The deception doesn't stop there, though. Hell, David has been deceiving his boss all year. The way he sits in the front at meetings—questioning and participating—he's actually led his boss to believe he's a great contribution to the company. His boss greets him as his "star worker," when in reality, David has done barely any work at all.

Perhaps David's slyest move of all happens as he sits in the meeting the day the presentations are due. Pretending he is in the same situation as his colleagues, David manages to find out what they wrote about so he can then use those ideas for his own presentation.

You need to be clever and cunning or your bullshit won't survive. It's not enough simply to lie. That doesn't make you more special than anyone else. It's all about the way you lie and the way you keep that lie alive and flourishing. A Bullshit Artist is a master in the art of manipulation and deception.

5. David Was Articulate

Words are your friends. If you can't articulate your bullshit, you're going to have a hard time making people believe what you're saying is true. The way you speak depends on what you want to get out of the situation. You might think there are some instances when it would be more appropriate to take the bumbling-fool approach, inserting "Ums" and "Uhs" throughout your sentences, but this is rarely the case.

Even though he acts nervous, David is always very clear about what he has to convey. He acts nervous because that's what his bullshit demands.

But what if David had taken the bumbling-fool approach? What if he had stumbled over his words? Would he still have gotten his boss to give him the extension? Well, maybe. Or, perhaps his boss would not have been as responsive to this method. Perhaps his boss would have seen David as the guilty party and become apathetic towards him. He should have done the work. Why should anyone have any pity for David? By bumbling and appearing nervous, David would appear small. But by speaking frankly and clearly, David is seen as someone strong and worthy of the boss's time.

If you stumble over your words, you'll either come off as unsure, or worse, you'll look like you are making it up on the spot (which you might very well be doing, but no one should know that). You need to be believable with what you say.

You don't need to study the dictionary and use long, convoluted words. Just be clear and speak with conviction. You need to prove you know *exactly* what you're talking about.

The way you speak to someone plays a huge role in making your bullshit believable. So make sure you're clear.

6. David Was Confident

When misrepresenting yourself, you absolutely, positively need confidence. Just as you can't appear nervous when speaking, you can't appear nervous in your mannerisms either. No fidgeting and no darting eyes. You need to be in a mindset where you have absolute confidence in what you are about to do—both before and while doing it. Confidence is why you remain calm and it's why you express yourself articulately. You do all of these things so that you can be in the moment and remain confident in the task at hand. Nothing, and I mean nothing, can turn Successful Bullshit into Spewed Shit quicker than a lack of confidence.

What if David had freaked out when he realized his presentation was due in mere hours? Would he have been able to compose himself enough to prepare for the upcoming bullshit session? Would he have been able to talk to his boss and make the boss believe that what David was saying was true?

Confidence is key to any true Bullshit Artist. If you aren't confident, I guarantee your bullshit will fail.

Confidence is very different from cockiness, and you shouldn't confuse the two. Sure, sometimes you need to be cocky, but not always. It depends entirely on the situation. Sometimes cockiness does more harm than anything else. If David had burst into his boss's office with a cocky attitude, he wouldn't have gotten very far, especially if he wanted his boss to do something for him.

You may know you're the shit, but it's not always best to let others in on that. Judge the situation. If the situation calls for cockiness, then go for it. Just make sure it's appropriate to your bullshit.

7. David Was Charming

It's really important that you come across as likeable when you're bullshitting someone. People are much more willing to do something for someone they like than for someone they despise.

Let this be your new mantra: *If you want your bullshit to work, don't act like a jerk.*

David doesn't barge into his boss's office and whine. He doesn't brag to his peers about the extension he received. Sure, you're taking advantage of people, but you don't want *them* to know that. Being charming is the cherry on top of any good bullshit sundae. According to Logan Pearsall Smith, "Charming people live up to the very edge of their charm, and behave as outrageously as the world lets them." Now charm the pants off the person you're bullshitting so they fall for it. It's amazing how far a smile will get you—especially when you have no idea what you're talking about.

8. David Was Attentive

Bullshit is never a solo activity. If you have a bullshitter, that also means you have a bullshitee, i.e., the person or persons that you bullshit. You should always treat your bullshit like a dialogue.

When having a dialogue or conversation with someone, you respond and react to what they are saying. In many ways, it's like playing a game of tennis. Ideas, thoughts, and reactions are the tennis balls that bounce from player to player. Player One says something, which sends the ball to Player Two. That person then responds, sending the ball back to Player One.

As previously mentioned, it's all right to go into a situation with your bullshit already planned, but don't make it so concrete that you can't adjust as the game unfolds. Take in your surroundings and be attentive. Often when a person is in the middle of a lie, he doesn't pay attention to the other person because he is so consumed with trying to remember his story. As a Bullshit Artist, you always need to be prepared to hit the tennis ball back to your "opponent" at any time. You might have to alter slightly the way you approach your BS, given what the other person is saying, so it's crucial that you remain attentive.

> Your bullshit is not a monologue.

Timing is crucial to being attentive. Always be alert and wait for the perfect moment to unleash your bullshit. Pay close attention to the other person, and if it feels right, let your BS seep into the conversation naturally. If you start your bullshit too soon, it will feel forced and the other person will notice.

Notice how attentive David is in the example. Immediately, he sets the tone when he enters his boss's office. As soon as his boss asks if everything is all right, David knows exactly how to respond so as to work his bullshit into the conversation. He pays close attention to his boss's reaction, and when he feels the moment is just right, he lets his bullshit fly. By being attentive and understanding his situation, he decides when to stand and attempt to leave. And he executes the maneuver perfectly. It's not enough just to have a good story to tell. It's also about timing.

9. David Was Dishonest

Ah, the no-brainer, right? Without being dishonest you can't bullshit. It is the Bernie Madoff to our Ponzi scheme. You won't get to the latter if you don't have the former.

Why, then, is dishonesty so far down on this list?

Well, lying is actually the easy part. Anyone can do it. Being able to lie doesn't make you any different from the guy sitting next to you on the bus, the old lady upstairs who takes your mail, or even your mother for that matter. ("No, Honey. We always planned on having another baby.")

A Bullshit Artist isn't just someone who can lie. A Bullshit Artist is someone who's got the system beat. A true Bullshit Artist can make a lie so believable that the other person never doubts it's anything but the absolute truth. That is why the other eight steps are so crucial. Treat these as your follow-up to the lie.

> Dishonesty is the foundation for Successful Bullshit, and a damn good one, but it's not everything you need in order to succeed.

On its own, lying is meaningless. It's just a group of words strung out in a sentence with no value to it. I can tell you I have six noses, when I don't. I can tell you I have a unibrow that connects to my sideburns, when I don't. I can tell you my earlobes hang down to the floor, when they don't. I can *say* all of these things (and be one hideous looking creature), but none of them mean anything unless there is a real value behind the words. Your job is to say the words and fake the value.

It's also important to distinguish something. The goal here is not to be a pathological liar. You want to say "Yes" to everything you should say "No" to—be my guest, but that's not going to make you a Bullshit Artist (although it will subsequently make you a bad Jim Carrey movie). Remember what I said in the first chapter, a Bullshit Artist uses bullshit to better himself.

Don't lie for the sake of lying. Then you're just spewing shit.

10. David Was Cautious

Last but not least, there's caution. You need to be careful when you are bullshitting. I can't stress enough how important this is. Nothing will turn your Successful Bullshit into Spewed Shit faster than not being cautious.

It should be obvious, but it deserves to be pointed out—don't forget your story. As Roman rhetorician Quintilian so aptly put it, "A liar should have a good memory." If halfway through your bullshit you can't remember what you said earlier, all of that hard work will transform into Spewed Shit.

Unfortunately, beyond that bit of advice, there is no tried-and-true formula that guarantees you are being cautious enough. You have to be able to feel out the situation and use common sense. With time and practice (or enough failures), it'll come to you. You are the best judge when it comes to these things. How is the other person reacting? Does it seem like they believe you? Are you going too far? Can you take it further? What's the next step? When should I do it? Ask yourself these questions when you're bullshitting and use the other nine characteristics to reinforce your bullshit.

Test the waters. If you think it's deep enough and feels right, dive in. If it seems a bit shallow, get your feet a little wet and ease into the water slowly. Don't be afraid to turn back around either. If you need to backtrack, and your bullshit permits it, then go for it.

> NOTE: Backtracking will get trickier the further you go into your bullshit and eventually, you might not be able to turn around. Do you have a backup plan? Can you fix your bullshit before it's too late?

The Takeaway

Successful Bullshit is an intense balancing act. You want to use your imagination and be creative, but you can't go overboard. You need to have some ballsiness, but too much and you'll look like a jerk. You need to remain calm, but a little pressure is always good to keep you in check. Be sly, but don't be sleazy. You need to be articulate, but sometimes, by being too articulate or not articulate enough, it will become obvious you're lying. You need confidence, but you can't get cocky. Be charming, but don't come across as fake.

Be attentive, use your dishonesty to your advantage, and be cautious. That's what differentiates a Bullshit Artist from any ol' person who can lie.

Can These Topics Help Me If I Don't Know Anything about the Topic?

Yes.

Let me explain. This is the perfect place to create bullshit. How many times have you been stuck in a situation while the conversation flies over your head? Or times when you speak so infrequently that all you ever manage to get out are a few "Ohs" and "Uhs"? Maybe you nod your head in agreement every now and then, but it's only out of pure desperation. You still have no idea what's going on and they could be speaking another language for all you know. Meanwhile, the other people in the room are probably starting to wonder who invited the bobble-head to this shindig in the first place.

Now, you no longer have to stare blankly ahead with that look of confusion on your face as you insert your two cents worth of monosyllabic noises. You can use bullshit and actually *engage* in conversation with these people. Hell, if you do it right, you could even *lead* the conversation. Well, at least that's how it will appear, and that's all that really matters. Make them think they're following *you* for a change.

> So much of bullshit is about how you present yourself.

It might seem impossible but trust me, it isn't. Don't be intimidated. No person is so good that you can't bullshit them. You know what it takes to do it. Think back to the characteristics of a successful bullshitter. How can you coerce information out of the other person without getting caught? Be ballsy, be cautious, and take control.

If you're charming enough, people will want to give you the information. You've got to be the guy in the room that everyone loves talking to. People need to feel like they're missing out if they're not talking to you. You've got to be *that* guy. Be engaging, be witty, be funny, be clever—and wait for them to provide you the information.

Once you get the hang of bullshitting, you'll gradually get more and more successful at it. Bullshit, like everything else worth doing, requires practice. If you do that, all of the pieces will fall into place. The characteristics won't seem like a long list you have to remember; they'll come to you naturally. If you don't get it the first time (and chances are you won't), that's okay. Pick yourself up and try again. Successful Bullshit is not easy—but when it's done right, it's one of the greatest feelings of accomplishment a person can have.

SAMPLE QUESTIONS:

1. How do you know when you've bullshitted successfully?
   A. You achieved your goal without anyone uncovering your lies.
   B. You were able to have a conversation you never thought possible by operating under false pretenses.
   C. You were able to achieve success more quickly by misrepresenting yourself.
   D. All of the above.

2. Which of the following is *not* a characteristic of a successful bullshitter?
   A. Articulate
   B. Calm
   C. Displeasing
   D. Cautious

3. *True or False?* I don't have to know anything about a subject to make someone think I do.

ANSWERS:

1. D
2. C
3. Seriously? Do I have to answer this?

QUESTIONS TO ASK YOURSELF:

- Why does Successful Bullshit work?
- What's motivating you to succeed?
- What are the ten characteristics of a successful bullshitter?
- What makes bullshit different from a lie?
- In what ways do you need to be cautious when bullshitting?
- Who invented bobble-head dolls anyway?

Don't think just because you know what it takes to be a good bullshitter, you will be one. You can get there, but it takes a lot of hard work and effort. Going through the motions of Successful Bullshit is like riding a bike—into a freeway. You must always be on your guard and peddling as fast as you can.

Chapter 3

How to Bullshit

"Genius [is] the ability to produce fantastic amounts of equally fantastic bullshit that all makes perfect sense."

—JASON ZEBEHAZY

Congratulations on making it this far and trying to master the art form that is bullshit. As a reward, here's the moment you've been waiting for. With all of the warnings and formalities out of the way, you can finally start learning how to BS. This is where you will be provided with tips, techniques, and exercises for you to use in your training. You are one giant step closer to becoming a Bullshit Artist. Make sure your shoes are tied and your arches are supported.

DISCLAIMER: Just like those 8-Minute Tae Bo Workout VHS tapes you own, this book is meant to be instructional. Unlike those 8-Minute Tae Bo Workout VHS tapes you own, *The Bullsh*t Artist* is meant to be used and not collect dust in your basement. Your results depend entirely on how much work you put in. A novice bullshitter is much like an Amish youth during rumspringa. There's a lot of information to take in from this new world, so it's best to go slowly. Stay a while and adjust to the automobiles and premarital sex—I mean, practice. Stay a while and practice.

And finally, before you begin . . . remember the ten characteristics of a successful bullshitter. These will come up throughout this chapter.

Tips, Techniques, and Exercises for Successful Bullshitting

Here's what you'll need for the following chapter:
- This book (obviously)
- A pen and notebook
- A voice recorder
- Unsuspecting test subjects

(NOTE: Some of the following exercises can be performed simultaneously.)

THE TIP: Maintain the Right Amount of Eye Contact

You can bullshit in many different arenas and with many different people. Bullshitting your boss and bullshitting the barista at your local coffee shop can (and probably should) play out in two very different ways. Similarly, *how you look* at a person can and should change from situation to situation. Maintaining the right kind of eye contact with the person you are about to bullshit is crucial to your success. You must use your eyes to sell yourself and make the other person want to believe anything you tell them.

> It's been said that eyes are the gateway to one's soul. If this is the case, make sure no one gets past the waiting room.

Eye contact plays a vital role in communication. With your eyes alone, you can express a range of emotions including happiness, anger, remorse, confidence, sincerity, and intimacy. But your eyes can also give you away.

Convincing someone to believe you isn't as simple as staring into her baby blues. Countless studies detail the significance of eye movement in conversation. Some studies suggest that a person will *avoid* direct eye contact when lying. To counteract this, people often attempt to maintain almost constant eye contact, fixing their eyes on the other person in a strange, "I want to look away but my eyes are frozen" manner. This will, in effect, lead them to overstay their eye-to-eye welcome. Keeping your eyes fixed on the other person for too long can seem unnatural and that can lead to discomfort and suspicion.

In other words, too little eye contact and you'll look like a liar. Too much eye contact and you'll look like a freak. In both cases, your BS fails.

Your eyes react to certain responses. In remembering a sound versus remembering an image, your eyes will move in different directions. Typically, if you are right-handed, when you make something up, your eyes will move to the right. If you are remembering something, your eyes will often move to the left (if you are left-handed, the reverse will be true). Of course, this does not apply to everyone, but enough evidence backs this theory.

Too much blinking, darting, and squinting are also dead giveaways that you're being dishonest. These mannerisms show the other person that either you're trying to hide something from them or you're nervous.

There are, of course, other meanings associated with eye movement. For instance, even though blinking can make you appear nervous, it can also be a sign of flirtation (which you might be able to use to your advantage under certain bullshitting scenarios). Similarly, extended eye contact can also be a sign of affection. These examples might seem contradictory to what was mentioned earlier, but it all depends on your specific situation.

To be considered a genuine Bullshit Artist, you must have the ability to bullshit anyone. For some people, you can get by with the right amount of eye contact and a normal number of blinks. When you face someone with more advanced lie-detecting abilities, however, you can use these tips (and again remember, lefties will do the reverse):

- Looking to the right suggests that you are creating an auditory thought (example: thinking how your roommate might scream if she were to see a mouse in your apartment).
- Looking down and to the right indicates you are creating a sensory thought (example: asking your roommate to think about how it felt when the mousetrap she attempted to set snapped on her finger).
- Looking up and to the right suggests creating an image visually (example: picturing your roommate running into the next room when she sees a mouse).
- Looking to the left suggests remembering something auditory (example: thinking about the sound of your roommate's shrieking when she actually saw the mouse approach her).

- Looking up and to the left indicates a visual image being remembered (example: remembering your roommate running into the wall and falling to the floor).
- Looking down and to the left usually shows you are talking to yourself (example: your roommate muttering to herself as she sits on the couch holding an icepack to her head).

THE TECHNIQUE: Use Your Peepers

Find the perfect balance between eye contact and no eye contact. Don't blink too much or dart your eyes; remain calm, and avoid the different indications that you are lying.

THE EXERCISE: Eyes, Eyes, Baby

Start out simply. Go to your local café, bar, mall, what have you, and do a little people watching. In order to trick the common man, you must first learn his behavior. Find two people in conversation. Where do their eyes move when they are talking? How much eye contact do they hold? Can you notice any of the signs of lying? Do their eyes shift or move to the right when they speak? Do they stare straight ahead or avoid eye contact?

Your first step is just to notice how eyes act in their natural environment. And if you spot a liar, make a note of it. After all, if you can tell they're lying, they're not very good at it. You have the opportunity to learn from their mistakes.

Now it's your turn. Start having conversations with people in your everyday life. Don't bullshit yet, just be yourself and talk. Talk to everyone you can. While you do so, pay close attention to your eye movement. How much eye contact do you make? When do you look away? When does the other person look away? Before you can introduce any sort of lying, you must understand your own behavior.

From here, start introducing lies—nothing major and nothing too obvious. If you don't know the bullshitee that well, maybe casually throw in a brother you don't have, or perhaps a college you never attended. If you do know the other person well, try to keep your lies somewhat realistic. If you hate shopping and never go, don't tell your best friend you love shopping and go all the time. Instead, maybe talk about a restaurant that you "went" to the other night, or a TV show you "saw."

Keep the lies small and uneventful. What's happening with your eyes? Pay close attention to this. How much eye contact have you been making? Think about the indicators of lying as you do so, and try to avoid betraying yourself.

Being self-aware of your eye movements will seem hard at first. It's akin to when someone thinks about his or her breathing, and as a result, their breathing changes. If you have never experienced this before, try it. Changing back and forth from involuntary to voluntary actions will help you become more self-aware of your body. And that knowledge will most certainly come in handy as a Bullshit Artist. Once you are aware of how and when your eyes move, begin the training process.

If your eyes move to the right when you start to lie, start moving them back to the person you are addressing. If you avoid eye contact, get back up there and look at the other person. And remember not to stare.

It's crucial you start training your eyes with these small, unimportant lies so that eye movements won't be as much of an issue when you're onto bigger and better fabrications.

Gradually, start upping the ante. Make your lies larger, longer, and more complex. As you do, always remain aware of your eyes. With enough practice, they will react no differently than they did with the smaller lies.

The Bare Minimum: At the very least, it's always best to look at the person you are bullshitting than to avoid eye contact. If you can't master how long is too long, at least you'll be able to make sure the other person is paying attention.

Characteristics: You Will Be: Calm, Confident, Attentive, Cautious

THE TIP: Sound Believable

What you say and how you say it are two very different things that need to be handled separately (and for the purposes of this chapter, will be). Remember, characteristics of a successful bullshitter include being calm, articulate, and charming. Your voice is one of the key players in getting your bullshit across and (quite obviously) it's the only thing the other person will hear. It is essential that you use your voice to help you instead of hurt you.

You might be saying the right words, but if the voice doesn't match, you're going up Shit Creek without a paddle.

Physiologically speaking, when people lie, their vocal chords actually tighten. This tightening, unfortunately for us bullshitters, is an involuntary action as a result of years of being told that lying is bad and the wrong thing to do. After entire childhoods hearing about a boy puppet with a nose complex, a boy who cries wolf, and a little chicken worried about sky-dandruff, the notion that lying is bad is ingrained in each and every one of us. And it's not going away any time soon.

No matter how you may feel now, your brain remembers and recognizes that you are doing something "bad" and reflexively your throat muscles tense.

When a person starts to lie, the tightening of the muscles becomes evident in his voice, and typically one of two things happen. Either the pitch of a person's voice gets higher, or his voice sounds gravelly, almost raspy, due to the lack of oxygen flowing through the throat. Another result of throat-muscle constriction and lack of airflow is frequent clearing of the throat.

Other major indicators of lying include speaking at an increased rate (related to being nervous), or speaking too slowly (because you're making up the story as you go along). Inserting a lot of "Ums" and "Uhs" in your sentence or quickly changing the subject also indicates that you are nervous, lying, or stalling for time. If you must change the subject, be subtle about it.

Think back to the characteristics of a successful bullshitter and remember that you need to remain calm. If you let nerves get the better of you, your bullshit dies instantly. Fear and nerves are something that we, as Bullshit Artists, need to cope with and fight. You need to sound normal.

THE TECHNIQUE: Make Your Voice Heard—and Believable

Control the speed and pitch of your voice when lying. The tricky thing about your voice when it comes to lying is that you have to sound exactly as you would in a "normal" conversation. This way, you sound believable and there's no reason for anyone to question you. Any change in tone or pitch raises red flags.

THE EXERCISE: Pick Up Good Vibrations

Reading the tip and technique might seem a bit frightening. You might wonder to yourself, "How am I supposed to control an involuntary response in my throat?"

Like any science experiment, you need to have a test sample and a control. In this case, your control is your normal speaking voice. In order to succeed, you must become very aware of how you actually talk to people. You need to have a good understanding of the basic tones, speed, and variations in your voice before you can start to experiment and change it.

The best way to fully understand your voice is simply by listening and studying it. Using your voice recorder, record normal conversations you have on a daily basis with someone whom you are both familiar and comfortable.

For the purposes of this exercise, it's always better to listen to how you speak in actual conversations as opposed to reciting a monologue to yourself in front of a mirror. Talking to yourself, whether in the privacy of your own home or somewhere more public, will not have the same effect as conversing with another person (you'll just come across as creepy).

This one-on-one time will help you better understand how your voice sounds, but will also help you learn how effective you are. Do you have a tendency to ramble? Or are you more precise when you talk with others? When interacting with another person, you play off each other in ways you simply wouldn't be able to if you were alone.

Study your voice. Typically, when we speak with someone we like, we are much more animated and far more engaged in the conversation and it comes across as such.

Record three to five conversations (to begin with, and then more if necessary) between you and your friends before even starting to incorporate any sort of bullshit into the equation. If it happens naturally, so be it, but don't force anything. It's important that these conversations are as comfortable as possible so that your voice can come out in its natural state.

Listen to the "real" you, so when you're faking it, you can replicate it.

While listening to the recordings afterward, have a pen and paper handy and take notes. Don't get all judgmental about how weird your voice sounds when it's recorded (even though it is). Instead, here's what you need to take away from the experiment:

- What is the basic tone of your voice?
- When does your voice get higher in pitch?
- When does it get lower?
- What is the basic speed when you speak?
- Are you fast or slow?
- Does the rate speed up at any point?
- Does it slow down at any point?
- What causes this variation? Does it have to do with what is being said?
- Do you stumble over your words at any point in the conversation?
- Do you get your message across clearly and effectively?

Make note of any other ideas you think might be interesting or beneficial regarding your voice. You might have to perform this part of the exercise several times in order to really get a good grasp of your voice qualities. Once you feel you have a good understanding of your voice, you can move forward with the rest of the exercise.

The next step is what I like to call "mental ambushing." To begin, this will require you to work outside of your circle of friends. I'm talking about strangers. Everyday people make the perfect lab rats.

You will never see any of these people again and you can tell them practically anything you want without consequence (unless it incurs police involvement; there are *some* limits to what you should say). Really let loose on these unsuspecting bystanders. Don't be afraid to take chances. This is where you can truly screw up without any fear of repercussions.

Begin the mental ambushing process by telling stories. I'm talking long, "Oh, one other thing"—keep them there for an hour longer—stories. What you say in these stories doesn't necessarily have to be true. If you feel comfortable with fabricating at this stage, then you absolutely should. The key part here is that you keep talking. And talking. And talking. You're looking for the gift of gab with a no return policy.

Why talk to random strangers for extended periods of time?

You need to get used to talking in front of others. It's crucial for your success. You may never have to bullshit someone for an hour straight, but being comfortable with the process will ensure that if you have to, you won't struggle. The second benefit to mental ambushing is that you'll begin to understand the importance of timing.

This trait goes back to the characteristic of being attentive. Every person has a limit to how much talking he can handle. Some people tolerate talkers, others, not so much. If you're attentive, you should recognize signs in the face and body gestures that signal when enough is enough.

With mental ambushing, even when you see the signs, keep laying it on. Because only when you feel comfortable speaking to people, can you really dive into the bullshitting process.

> Your voice is your instrument. If you want to sing the opera known as Successful Bullshit, then you'd better sound like a freakin' Pavarotti.

Consider this. Without sparking a debate about politics or bringing up previous romantic endeavors that turned sour, can you think of some of the greatest liars around today? Here are just a few that come to mind:

- Meryl Streep
- Robert De Niro
- Sean Penn
- Daniel Day-Lewis
- Al Pacino

What do you notice about these people? Yep, they're all actors. Talented actors have the uncanny ability to make you believe they really are the person they are portraying. They are able to misrepresent themselves and entirely accept this new identity as their own. And if they're good, we believe them. Hell, we even go so far as to hand out awards when they've done it particularly well.

Bullshit Artists are actors, too. And just as we know when an actor does a terrible job, so too can we recognize when someone spews shit.

The truly amazing thing about these actors, though, isn't that they can memorize lines and recite them on cue. They're truly impressive because they can express a wide range of emotions and make it completely believable. Here you see a perfect case of people completely lying their asses off, with no vocal indications to give them away. How do they do that?

Many talented actors use Method Acting. The term has branched out over the years into several different schools of thought, but the main idea behind all of them is an actor creates a lifelike performance through the creation of thoughts and feelings her character would experience if she were a real person. Where normal acting classes focus on how an actor appears on the outside, Method Acting urges students to internalize the process. By focusing on what is inside, what appears on the outside becomes much more believable.

Now, don't get me wrong. I'm not telling you to become a method actor. (Who wants all those awards, am I right?) But there is something to be said about Method Acting and how successful the process is. How these people can turn something so fictional into something so believable is an incredible talent—and *any* liar can learn a thing to two from these folks.

And what about your throat? Does any of this internalizing really keep the muscles in your throat from tightening? Well, it could, if you practiced enough. But more importantly, your bullshit will still sound believable even if you can't control your throat muscles.

Another helpful hint is to have a drink on you when it's appropriate. Don't run to the kitchen to grab a glass of water the moment you're going to start bullshitting, but if you're at a bar, have a drink in your hand and *sip casually*. This will lubricate your throat when need be, and give you a prop to hold so you don't start to fidget. Be careful not to rely on the drink as a form of protection.

The Bare Minimum: If you take one thing away from this exercise, it should be this: the very least you can do to keep your voice believable is to keep it at a steady tone and pace. Alterations in pitch and rhythm can come across as suspicious.

Characteristics: You Will Be: Ballsy, Calm, Sly, Articulate, Confident, Charming, Attentive, Cautious

HISTORICAL MOMENT OF SPEWED SHIT
CAITLIN UPTON, MISS TEEN SOUTH CAROLINA, 2007

WHAT SHE SAID: "I personally believe that U.S. Americans are unable to do so because, uh, some people out there in our nation don't have maps. And I believe that our education like such as in South Africa and, uh, the Iraq everywhere like, such as. And I believe that they should, our education over here in the U.S. should help the U.S., or, should help South Africa and should help the Iraq and the Asian countries, so we will be able to build up our future for our children."

WHAT SHE MEANT: "You know, I honestly don't have a clue."

THE TIP: Get Into Bodybuilding

We're not talking six packs and dumbbells, here. The way you present yourself physically impacts your bullshit. What's worse, if you aren't comfortable in your own skin, that can tip off a person they're being bullshitted before you even get any words out of your mouth.

First and foremost, there's fidgeting. Fidgeting is tricky because it can go unnoticed by the bullshitter while the other person will see it clear as day. Fidgeting includes things like shuffling around, putting your hand through your hair, biting your nails, biting your lip—all of those little habits you do out of nervousness that you may not even realize. These little signs tell the other person "something isn't as it seems."

Fidgeting breaks the trust you have tried so hard to develop and maintain with the other person. When she sees you fidget, she loses interest in anything else you have to say. It tells her you aren't confident. As a Bullshit Artist, you can never let that happen.

Much like in the case of eye contact, when a person might force him or herself to stare intently at the other person to prove they aren't lying, body language, too, can be overdone. People tend to think that, in order to prove they aren't lying, they must have very open body language. The end result is an exaggeration that comes off as extremely fake. If you succumb, you jeopardize your bullshit. Whatever you do, don't overthink your body language. You want to appear natural. Make like Mae West who supposedly said, "I speak two languages, Body and English."

To help you better understand body language, keep in mind these help-ful tips:

- If a person's head is tilted, it shows interest
- An occasional nodding of the head indicates that a person is paying attention, but too much can indicate the person is not actually listening
- Standing with your arms folded tends to mean you are closed off
- If the other person mirrors your body movements, it shows interest
- If the other person's eyes are drifting, it shows boredom
- If the other person comes close to you or touches you, it shows intimacy
- Using your hands to talk gives you less of a chance to fidget
- Standing up straight shows confidence
- Tapping of the feet or hands shows impatience
- Loose arms show that you are relaxed
- Sweating shows that you are nervous

You would think this last tip I am going to share would be common sense, but it would not be fair of me to exclude it. It's still very important for you to be aware of if you wish to succeed.

Dress Appropriately

If you are trying to bullshit your boss for a raise, it might not be the best idea to wear a T-shirt, jeans, and flip-flops. If you know you sweat when you are nervous, don't wear something that will make you hot. If you want to appear comfortable, you should at least *be* physically comfortable.

Your wardrobe should be the final piece that puts your bullshit together. Don't allow it to take away from all your hard work.

THE TECHNIQUE: Learn to Surf, Not Body Bored

Good body language is all about being open. The other person is more apt to believe you if you come across as friendly, engaging, and ready to listen. Do not demonstrate physical indications that you're lying; instead invite conversation with your body language. Make sure not to close the other person off in any way.

THE EXERCISE: Invasion of the Body Snapshot

Once again, your first step is to observe. It might seem redundant, but remember, you are out to trick and deceive people. It only makes sense that you study them to understand better what you can and can't get away with—or can and can't do.

For this exercise you can go anywhere, but I suggest social places such as bars, clubs, parks, or malls. What you're looking for is people. Lots of people. People with other people. At this stage, you're going to want to be somewhere where a person's entire body is exposed. Restaurants and cafés are not the most ideal locations for this exercise because people are sitting. You want to take in the actions of the whole body, not be limited to above the waist.

Look around you and find a conversation between two people. Position yourself far enough away so that two things can happen:

1. You have a good view of both of their bodies.
2. You can't hear what they are saying.

If not in a club or loud environment, I recommend listening to music while doing this. For this exercise to work, it's important that there is absolutely no chance you will hear what these people are saying. The actual words are not important. It's the way their bodies speak that matters.

Your first task is just to observe the body language of the people talking.

- What's happening with their bodies?
- Is one person more dominant than the other?
- How do their bodies change when they are talking?
- How do their bodies change when they are listening?
- What seems to be the overall mood of the conversation?
- Do they both seem comfortable with each other?
- What do their arms and hands do?
- What do their legs and feet do?
- Where do they position their heads?

Recall the discussion about body language, and try to piece together the relationship between these two people. This might seem hard, but once you get the hang of it, it's rather easy. Focus on the big ideas. Start by asking yourself these questions. And of course, these are just guesses. But make them educated guesses based on the series of facts that you have observed.

- How do they know each other?
- What about the way they position their bodies tells you that?
- What are they talking about?
- Are they both being honest?
- What about their body language tells you that?

Do this several times until you feel you have a good understanding of how body language works. Make note of what you think is good, over-bearing, false, or all-around creepy. Also make note of the things you see repeated from sample to sample.

Now it's your turn to start applying these ideas into real-world situations. The more you get to talk to people, the more you can hone your body language. Become familiar with how your body works. Are you open? Are you closed off? What do you do with your arms and legs? Can you be more engaging? What can you improve?

In many ways body language is like a steak; it's better when little is done to it and worse when it's overcooked. That's not to say you shouldn't try to improve the steak with a little salt and pepper here and there, but you want to focus on bringing out its natural flavors.

Your goal is to be as normal and engaging as possible, so it's best not to trace out and analyze every movement you make. If you think you can be more open in the situation, then make a minor adjustment. Don't try too hard or it will come across as awkward or forced, and the other person will notice it right away. If you are a more closed-off person, start changing slowly. Maybe keep your hands out of your pockets for an entire night out. The next time, start to use your hands more in conversation. Build on the work you have already done.

Once you feel comfortable with your body, you can start to introduce your bullshit. Remember, if you are comfortable and engaging, the other person will be much more inclined to believe you.

Never underestimate the power of body language and appearance.

On September 26, 1960, John F. Kennedy and Richard Nixon (an infamous shit spewer) faced off in the world's first televised presidential debate. Those who had tuned into the debate via radio believed Nixon to be the stronger candidate. However, those who viewed the debate on television saw the young Kennedy as the clear winner of the night.

Why the discrepancy? If you listened to the debate on the radio, Nixon sounded far more experienced than Kennedy. But if you watched the debate on TV, you found yourself looking at two very different men. There was Kennedy, the young, calm, and handsome candidate who seemed comfortable under the bright lights; and then there was Nixon, the pale, sweaty, and intense incumbent who didn't appear comfortable in the slightest.

The debate changed television as a news medium and altered how the American audience viewed their political figures. And, you know, John F. Kennedy became the thirty-fifth president of the United States and one of the most beloved and revered political figures in American history. So there's also that. . . .

The Bare Minimum: Dress in appropriate and comfortable clothing. Keep your body as open as you can, avoid crossing your arms and avoid any sort of fidgeting. Mirroring the other person's actions and talking with your hands are the best ways to show you are paying attention. When in doubt, don't overthink it. Just be in the moment and pay attention to the other person. You'll come across much calmer.

Characteristics: You Will Be: Calm, Sly, Confident, Charm, Attentive, Cautious

THE TIP: Stay Connected

We now have information literally at our fingertips at all times. Walk down any street and you will see people talking into their hands or into little squares clipped to the sides of their faces. Often, a person's stare is now fixed on a few fingers as he types away on the little box he's holding. When we hear a ring or beep or feel any sort of vibration, we immediately stop everything else we were doing, reach into our pockets, and pull out the source of the disruption.

Cell phones have become a part of everyone's day-to-day wardrobe and a norm, if not must-have, in today's society. And phones are no longer just calling devices. These are game changers in the world of bullshitting.

As technology evolves, so too must the Bullshit Artist. It happened when the Internet first came about, and it's happening right now. Information is becoming much more accessible and that makes catching a lie much easier. If you fear technology and avoid it, your bullshit will get blown out of the water (or worse, you'll look like your parents who still used dial-up for seven years even though they didn't have to). You need to understand what's happening technologically so you can use it to your advantage when bullshitting.

With the cell phone, particularly the smart phone, a bullshitter's job is made much harder. Essentially, if a person's phone can connect online, he has a lie detector in his pocket. If you lie to someone, that person can whip out a phone and verify what you just said. Your bullshit can unravel within seconds just from the click of a button or tap of a very complicated multitouch screen. And there's very little you can do about that (short of grabbing the phone and throwing it, which I don't recommend for liability's sake—and because you'll end up having to pay for a new phone).

To say the smart phone is a bullshit killer is incorrect. Though the smart phone can quickly turn your bullshit into Spewed Shit, it doesn't *have to be* a bullshit killer. Bullshit Artists still thrive with the ever-growing worldwide web of today, and will be able to continue their success even as smart phones get smarter.

If you are afraid your bullshit will be found out because of a phone, you need to handle your bullshit more carefully. Try not to throw around specific information like hard facts and figures unless you actually know them. If you fabricate facts, make sure the person buys into your bullshit without a shadow of a doubt. Any uncertainty might lead him to take out that phone of his, and if the reception's good, he'll soon be on the line with 1-800-SPEWED-SHIT.

THE TECHNIQUE: Smart Phony

Don't be afraid of that small computer. You need to harness the power of technology to enhance your bullshit, or be so good at bullshitting that she won't feel the need to take her phone out in the first place.

THE EXERCISE: Cell Yourself

You can't control the content on the cell phone, but you can control whether or not the person *looks* at his phone. Here's how.

Only hang out in places with poor reception. This is an exercise best performed in the moment right before you begin your bullshit. Start out by learning about the other person's phone habits. How is he using it? There are those people who hold on to their phone like a security blanket, and others who drop or lose it within the first fifteen minutes of being at a bar. Some people will spend an entire night using their phone for any reason imaginable, going out of their way to take it out, while others are more blasé, and don't care if their phone is at the other end of the room the whole night.

Learn how your target works. If she isn't much of a phone person, you're in the clear. If she is, be extra careful with how you approach your bullshit.

If you own your own smart phone and know in advance what you'll be bullshitting about, use your costly data plan and agile fingers to your advantage. Before entering a bullshitting situation, do some research and look into topics you might want to cover. Get to know a few quick facts to make your bullshit more believable. That way, if it seems like the other person doesn't trust what you are saying, you can always pull the "Oh, you don't believe me, huh? Check this out." Then direct her to the page and prove you're right.

If possible, let her find it on her phone. That way, she becomes part of the discovery process. After all, if you were simply to present the information, it might seem suspicious. You have to be careful it doesn't look like you just visited that site seconds before (which you did). By allowing the other person to discover the site, it lets her take some ownership and that helps establish a level of confidence and ultimately ups your game of BS.

> Remember, if you're believable and engaging enough, she won't want to check her phone in the first place.

Now, if you don't own a smart phone, that's okay. You can get through your bullshit without one (even if they are flashy, do cool things that are pointless, and have a high-resolution camera which you'll never need). Try to concentrate more on the characteristics of a successful bullshitter, and less on the hard facts unless you know them. Because a true Bullshit Artist is so good at deceiving people, it shouldn't matter whether the other person has a smart phone. If you're engaging and believable enough, the other people will listen and want to listen to you. They won't feel the need to fact check your every sentence.

The Bare Minimum: If you lack an intelligent phone, don't use hard facts unless you are absolutely sure your target is falling for your bullshit. If you do own a smart phone, use it to your advantage. When using it for research, make sure you don't get caught.

Characteristics: You Will Be: Sly, Articulate, Charming, Attentive, Cautious

THE TIP: Stay Sociabull Online

In keeping with the subject of technology for a moment, you need to be aware of three things when it comes to your bullshit:

- The person you're pretending to be
- The person you actually are (what you want to keep from the bullshitee)
- The person you are online

The buzzword in terms of technology these days is "social." Everyone wants to know what everyone else is doing and everyone wants to be in your business—*at all times*. A digital smorgasbord of pointless pieces of personal information hang out there, and we all feel the need to contribute to it.

If you expose too much information on social networking sites it can put your BS in jeopardy, and increase your chances of getting caught. But a social networking site can also be a valuable tool. If used correctly, these sites can provide useful information about the person you want to bullshit. In many ways, these sites are a bullshitter's dream come true! With the click of a button, you can view a person's interests and gain enough information to build your bullshit.

THE TECHNIQUE: URL (Ultra-Reliable Lie)

Maintain a smart and simple online persona. The devil is in the details and you need to make sure everything you put online is not going to hurt you in the long run.

THE EXERCISE: They Can't See Your Privates

This is a fairly straightforward exercise. Research the various privacy settings for the sites where you have a profile. Display only the information that you're absolutely sure will not hurt you in the long run.

Do you want everyone to see everything on your profiles? Do you have information there that should be kept private? Anything that could prompt someone to call you out on your BS should either be taken down—or you should at least limit who is privy to the full profile.

The Bare Minimum: Make sure all personal information on your profiles is limited and not too revealing. It's better to have a boring page than to be called out on your bullshit.

Characteristics: You Will Be: Sly, Attentive, Cautious

THE TIP: Say What?

So far, you've learned how to cover yourself in various ways so you don't appear as if you're bullshitting and you've learned the qualities it takes to make you a successful bullshitter. But what about what you actually say? What about the actual bullshit?

As we all know, any time you are going to bullshit, you are going to be dishonest. So to blast your BS into orbit, you need fuel. You've got to lie.

While each bullshitting scenario is different, there are certain tips that can help you in any situation.

- Know your audience before starting the lie.
- Build out the story of your lie.
- Remember your story—and stick to it.
- Use details.
- Be engaging.

- Use eye contact and body language to further convince others your story's legit.
- Believe your lie (for the time being).

Assuming you've read this far, you know by now that a Bullshit Artist uses bullshit to get something out of a situation. Blindly bullshitting is spewing shit, and that's what you want to prevent at all times. So before you begin the deception process, the first thing you need to do is know your audience and understand the dos and don'ts of the situation. Who are you going to be bullshitting? What will it take for them to believe you? A Bullshit Artist only has so much power. It's actually the audience that decides whether your bullshit lives or dies, so it's crucial that you know the profiles of your targets and understand how to speak their language.

Think to yourself:

- What will it take for the other people to believe me?
- How well do I know these people?
- How well do they know me?

If you are meeting people for the first time, it will be much easier to bullshit them. If you have previous experience with them, in order to be believable, your bullshit needs to match your character.

If your goal in lying is just to have one thing to say in case you are questioned about it, then you're not taking full advantage of all that bullshit has to offer. Your lie should be a work of art on its own. Think of lying as being an author to your very own story. For you to come off as believable, this story must have a beginning, middle, and an end.

Building up your story takes careful effort. Include small, minute details that seem otherwise irrelevant. Talk about the kind of shirt someone was wearing, or the smell of the room that reminded you of your grandmother's house. Don't ever be vague. Be clear and be specific. Little things will have a big effect on whether people believe your story. Detail is the glue that holds your story together. If you can bring in details throughout, it makes it seem more as if you're recalling a memory and less like you're making something up on the spot. But don't go overboard. People tend to shut down and roll their eyes when they hear something far-fetched. Your job as a Bullshit Artist is to keep your audience captivated the entire time.

You never want your lie to seem like it is told out of desperation (*especially* when it is). You need to be on your toes when bullshitting. This is why it's so important to have your story planned down to the fine details.

Once you've got the story, your next step is to stick to it and remember it. Michel de Montaigne had a point when he said, "He who is not very strong in memory should not meddle with lying." Remembering your lie is crucial for your bullshit's longevity. Hell, even if it's for one night, if someone asks you, "What was that thing you told me a half hour ago?" you'd better have an answer and you better not have to think about it. Your story needs to come naturally to you so you don't hesitate when asked a question. You can't stumble over your words—your story needs to feel like a real memory.

No matter what someone asks, have an answer ready. If your lie is not well thought out, you'll end up relying more heavily on the other tips and characteristics to help you get through the situation. In this case, balancing everything is the only way for your bullshit to truly succeed.

You must engage with the other person when you lie, especially if you don't remember your entire fabrication. Lay on the charm, and act friendly and attentive so the other person views you in a positive light—after all, she'll be more inclined to believe you if she likes you.

Lastly, even though this sounds contradictory, you must believe your lie. If you go into a conversation thinking, "I'm completely lying right now," your body language could give you away in the subtle ways we've discussed. However, if you're confident and actually believe your lie, your body is less apt to say differently. By being relaxed you'll have a much easier time coming up with responses to keep the lie spinning.

THE TECHNIQUE: Liar, Liar, Pants Are Fireproof

Make your lie so foolproof in its design that you won't be able to stumble over it should any curveballs be thrown your way. Prepare in great detail for your lie and show confidence that you know what you're saying. When it comes to a good lie, half the battle is selling yourself, so be prepared to go the distance with your lie. Some artists lead with their hearts, but Bullshit Artists lead with their brains.

THE EXERCISE: The Liar, the Witch, and the Wardrobe

In your notebook, start writing lies. Think of different scenarios either at home or at work, and think about how you might lie to someone. At this point, these don't have to be big lies and they don't even have to be all that believable. You just need to think of lies and put them on paper. The goal of this process is to get that brain of yours thinking about how lies are formed.

On a piece of paper, create an outline as follows:

The Lie:
The Purpose of the Lie:
The Beginning of the Lie:
The Middle of the Lie:
The End of the Lie:
The Details:

Here's an example for you.

The Lie: I've been eating healthier for three weeks now.

The Purpose of the Lie: To shut my girlfriend up.

The Beginning of the Lie: Three weeks ago, I took a look in the mirror and didn't like what I saw. Though my girlfriend had been telling me for quite some time that I should change my eating habits, the decision was entirely mine. I want to have a healthier lifestyle.

The Middle of the Lie: It was a bit hard at first to change my diet completely, but it soon got easier for me.

The End of the Lie: I feel much healthier as a result of this new diet.

The Details: There were a few times I fell off the bandwagon and ate something I wasn't supposed to (chips, cookies, carbs), but overall I've followed through with the diet and have been eating fruits and vegetables (asparagus, broccoli, green beans) with every meal. When my girlfriend comes over to my apartment, I will prepare her a healthy meal (a recipe I found online and have never had before) and tell her it's my favorite of the new meals I've been cooking for myself.

NOTE: Obviously, this is not the lie of a Bullshit Artist. A lie about dieting would only get you so far until the visual cues would start to disprove your story. Also, if you're going to lie to your girlfriend, unless you never share a meal with her, something like the food you eat would be nearly impossible to fake. But right now, just put that aside. This exercise isn't about what the lie is; it's about getting your creative juices flowing. Another good part about this experiment is that you'll be able to see for yourself what lies can—and cannot—work. Yes, this example is a lie, but it's not a good case for bullshitting.

Continue working on outlines like these. As you do, make them more and more applicable to your everyday life. Weed out the bad lies and begin to focus on lies that would make for good BS. Gradually eliminate the pen and paper and instead make mental outlines in your head.

Once you have mastered this process and understand how the outline works, you're ready to start introducing your lies to the real world. Start with small lies and work up to larger ones. As you lie to people, remember to include those extra details that ground it in "reality."

If you become familiar enough with this method, it'll become easier for you to create these stories. This will come in handy particularly when you need to lie off the top of your head—when you're not going into a situation with your bullshit already planned. Just because it is impromptu, doesn't mean you should treat it any differently. In situations like this, you'll have to rely on your ability to remain calm, your ability to build a story quickly, and your stellar memory.

The Bare Minimum: Whether on the spot or planned in advance, REMEMBER YOUR STORY! Your bullshit will get better with plenty of details, but it won't amount to a hill of beans if you can't recall what you were saying. If your memory isn't that great, don't make it too complicated.

Characteristics: You Will Use: All of them!

You may have noticed that this exercise requires all ten characteristics of a successful bullshitter. Remember to use those qualities as your guide to any good lie. They are all crucial to creating your bullshit—and making it stick.

SAMPLE QUESTIONS:

1. Why is eye contact so important when bullshitting?
2. Which of the following indicates you are lying?
   A. Your eyes shift to the right.
   B. You avoid eye contact entirely.
   C. You stare at the other person for too long.
   D. All of the above.

3. Physiologically speaking, what happens to your voice when you lie? Why does this happen?

4. Why do actors sound so believable?

5. Which of the following body movements indicate you are lying?

   A. Fidgeting

   B. Mirroring the body movements of the other person

   C. An occasional nod of the head while talking

   D. Being close to the other person while in conversation

6. Why should you be careful about what goes into your profile on a social network?

7. Why is it important to build out the story of your lie?

8. True or False? You can't successfully lie if you are making it up on the spot.

9. Does a smart phone come with the purchase of this book?

ANSWERS:

2. D

5. A

8. False, of course you can. You've just got to be extra careful in the way you build your story out and remember it.

9. What, are you nuts?

QUESTIONS TO ASK YOURSELF:

- How much eye contact do I make when I'm talking to someone?
- Does my voice get higher or lower when I'm nervous?
- What does my body language say about me? Am I a more open or closed person?
- Do I include enough details in my lies to make them believable?
- How creepy am I going to look when I'm watching all of these people?

As much as I love that you're reading this, simply *reading* these tips and exercises will only get you so far. If you want to be a true Bullshit Artist, you're going to have to get out there and put these to work. So put the book down for a second and start bullshitting!

Chapter 4

When to Bullshit

> "I'll always survive because I've got the right combination of wit, grit, and bullshit."
> —DON KING

You never know when the need could arise for good BS, so you should always be prepared. Your bullshitting skills are your Swiss Army knife; keep them handy and sharp just in case you need to pull them out.

So when and where should you bullshit? Any place and any time—life is full of bullshitting opportunities. Consider the situation. Study it and think back to your training. Remember the exercises and the characteristics of a successful bullshitter, and ask yourself, "Is this a good time to break out my bullshitting abilities? Can I get something out of this? Is my goal achievable? Is it worth the risk?" If you answer yes to all of these questions, then it's time to stop talking to yourself and get BS'ing.

But remember, a Bullshit Artist does *not* use bullshit whenever he feels like it. A Bullshit Artist uses bullshit any time there is something to gain.

> Once you become good at bullshitting, you will be able to dupe anyone. But there are some people you should maybe think twice about bullshitting.

Who you should never bullshit: Your doctors (there's no point in bullshitting a doctor; that's the only person who actually needs to know how you got that rash), and your lawyers (let them do the bullshitting for you, it's their job).

Who you should bullshit: Everyone else.

Think of your bullshit as a tiny organism. Some organisms only live and grow in very hot places; others in extremely cold places. Some survive in completely dark and damp areas, while others thrive in very sunny and arid locations. Creatures that live in the freezing tundra simply cannot survive in the dry desert and vice versa.

Your bullshit wants to breathe, grow, and flourish, and in order to do so, it has to adapt to its environment.

Situations When It's Best to Bullshit

If you want to best utilize your new craft, you need to understand the environment where your bullshit takes place. Where and when to bullshit should be broken down into three categories: Work Bullshit (WBS), Social Bullshit (SBS), and Other Bullshit (OBS).

Why the differentiation? Well, the success of each type of bullshit means you need to act according to the environment. Let's take a quick look at how each of these bullshit environments breaks down.

Work Bullshit (WBS)

Climbing the corporate ladder? Bullshit's your number one tool on your way to the top. Bullshit can get you the job you've always wanted, it can make you the boss's favorite, and it can even get you that promotion you had been hoping to get. For WBS, you just need the standard suit, tie, and briefcase packed with bullshit.

Bullshit in the work environment looks very different from Social Bullshit or Other Bullshit for obvious reasons. You may have creative or personal interests in mind, but at the end of the day, you're working for the dollar signs.

Work Bullshit is about finding the right way to suck up to your boss without coming across as obnoxious, fake, or a suck-up. Work Bullshit is about looking like you respect your boss while you fake him out. It's about looking like you respect your boss *so you can* fake him out.

And this isn't a one-time deal, either. To BS your superior takes daily commitment. After all, you'll be seeing this person for as long as you stay with the company. If you plan on making a name for yourself there, then we're talking about a bullshit press, Monday through Friday, nine to five—plus overtime.

For Work Bullshit to succeed, you must first make an impression on your boss. Become your boss's confidant. Study his behavior and find something that you can focus on to fine-tune your relationship. Be his buddy and make yourself his best line of defense. If he needs something done, put yourself out there and tell him you'll do it, especially if you can't or don't know how. Make it clear that you're his go-to person.

If you exercise your bullshitting skills with finesse, you will be able to get your coworkers to do the work for you. And all the while, your boss will think you're a go-getter and someone who gets things done. Look like the overachiever without overly achieving.

This brings us to the other important part about Work Bullshit, regarding how you treat your coworkers. As a working Bullshit Artist, you need to utilize the strengths and knowledge of the people around you so that you can then take advantage of those traits.

Gain their friendship and camaraderie. Show them you have what it takes to succeed and you're the guy they should want to know. These are the people you commiserate with on a hard day. It's fine to be chummy with the boss, but if the people you work with on a day-to-day basis don't like you, you're going to have a hard time putting on a happy face each morning. And you'll have an even harder time using their skills to your advantage. It'll be much easier to get the things you want if everyone likes you and is willing to help you out. Work BS with your coworkers entails building relationships so you can con them into doing whatever you need done.

There is a big difference here between Work Bullshit and being a brownnoser. Brownnosers are just pathetic bullshit wannabes who don't understand how the system works. As a Bullshit Artist, you must be well-liked by everyone, from the CEO of the company to the interns who get your coffee. You want to suck up, but you definitely don't want to *look* like a suck-up.

All it takes is one person seeing through your bullshit, and all of your hard work devolves into Spewed Shit. Put yourself out there, be charming, and be the guy everyone likes. Don't come across as insincere or fake.

WBS is the type of bullshit that helps you out of that stuffy cubicle, and into that freshly painted office with legroom and a view. It's about standing out as the most successful guy while still being the likeable guy everyone can depend on. Become part of the conversations around the workplace and make people think you can fix any problem that comes your way. And of course, use your coworkers' skills to your advantage.

Successful WBS is measured by the level of respect you have in your office (not necessarily *earned*) and more importantly, by the number of zeros in your paycheck. Once you get the hang of how WBS works, you can stop brown bagging lunch—the boss will be buying.

Who You Can Bullshit in the Workplace:
Your boss
Your coworkers
A sale

Perfect Bullshit Situations:
Getting a job/assignment
Getting a raise
Getting a promotion
Making a sale
Getting an extension
Talking around the water cooler
Getting your coworkers to do the work for you
Getting recognized by your boss or the higher-ups

Social Bullshit (SBS)

This bullshit allows any guy to get any girl in the bar. This is the power of sweet talking and charming the pants off people (sometimes literally). You know when people say, "How on earth did he get *her*?" Well, he did it with Social Bullshit. There are plenty of fish in the sea, and if you so desire, you can be the net that catches them all.

Social Bullshit is the bullshit you find in any type of social gathering. We're talking about dates, parties, bars, clubs, high school reunions, birthdays, ribbon-cutting ceremonies, bris parties (the *other* ribbon-cutting ceremony)—any place where people are being social and you have to talk. It's your chance to be that guy everyone wants to be around and no one can stop talking about. You want to be popular? You want everyone to know who you are? You want the friends and the hot girls by your side? You need to hone your SBS abilities. You are the sperm, your bullshit is the egg, and the result is the life of the party.

It's crucial that you remember the lessons on body language and how to read other people when in conversation. This is particularly true in situations where ~~one night stands~~ romance is involved. Be in tune with what she's saying in terms of both the words that come out of her mouth, and what her body tells you. Always remember to be attentive and adjust your bullshit as necessary.

Using what you know about bullshit, be interesting, be engaging, and be smart. Craft your bullshit so the other person simply can't stop talking to you. With WBS, there is a certain hierarchy you need to follow. Your priority is to please the boss, get the work done (by others), and collect your paycheck. With SBS, there isn't any necessary hierarchical order. This is about the power of one-on-one conversations and being too good to be ~~true~~ lying.

You can also use Social Bullshit as an escape from awkward situations and as a tool for small talk. Seeing the in-laws over the holiday? On a blind date? Forced into volunteering at a retirement home despite your fear of old people? You can get through it with ease using Social Bullshit.

Who You Can Bullshit in a Social Situation:
Potential soul mates you meet one night at a bar
Your date/boyfriend/girlfriend
Your friends
People at a party
Your in-laws/extended family
Any place where mingling is required

Perfect Bullshit Situations:
Talking about a subject when you know nothing
Making small talk
Getting out of an argument
Wooing the woman you want to ~~take home~~ date
Surviving awkward encounters
Becoming popular

Other Bullshit (OBS)

Other Bullshit allows you to achieve any other goals you might have outside of your WBS or SBS. If you want to negotiate a price on an already-discounted item, this is the bullshit you're going to use. If you want to talk your girlfriend into buying you that completely amazing and rather pointless shaved-ice machine, OBS is what you'll need. If you want to get out of going to your sister's ballet recital, jeté over to Other Bullshit.

When using Other Bullshit, it's all about having a smart, believable answer to get your way. Remember how great it felt when your parents let you play hooky, then called the school and told them you were sick? This is like that, but on a grander scheme.

With Other Bullshit, avoid making excuses; instead, act as if you have verifiable proof to back your claims. It's about sounding believable and embodying confidence in your position. You are the driver—and you always have the right of way.

Who You Can Bullshit When the Mood Strikes:
Anyone you come across

Perfect Bullshiting Situations:
Any time you want something to happen
Any time you want to get out of a situation

You'll often find that many times these types of bullshit intertwine with one another. Sometimes you'll need to use SBS skills when in the middle of OBS. Sometimes OBS pops up at your office in the middle of a conversation with a coworker. At the end of the day, bullshit is always changing, growing, and evolving, and you must always be willing to adapt to the process and environment. WBS, SBS, and OBS are merely the foundations of bullshitting opportunities. Just because it starts as one, doesn't mean it can't morph midstream.

Examples of Bullshitting in Action

In trying to understand successful BS, you need to see it in action. Now that we have a good grasp of the many environments in which bullshit can thrive, let's take a look at a few examples. Study these cases and learn from them—this is how good bullshit is done.

WORK BULLSHIT: Bullshitting Your Boss

The office is busy as usual, but Toby is not in the mood to be stuck in his cubicle all day. The sun is shining, and eighteen holes and a brand new nine iron are calling his name. Toby calls his friend and tells him to be at their favorite course in twenty minutes. He hangs up the phone and approaches his boss, explaining that he has just made plans to take a prospective client out to lunch. His boss has no reason to object. So far, so good.

Before you know it, Toby and his friend are out on the green, enjoying a beautiful day, and a slightly less beautiful golf game. On their way to the eighth hole, however, Toby hears a distinctive laugh coming from behind him. Turning around slowly so as not to draw attention, Toby catches a glimpse of his boss walking the green with the CEO of the company. His boss hasn't seen him yet—he could bolt now without ever getting caught. Instead, Toby walks right up to his boss, calling his name as he approaches.

His boss's mouth drops as Toby gets closer. *What the hell is he doing here?* Toby laughs at the coincidence and goes right into his spiel. He begins by introducing his golfing buddy to everyone, using an alias and informing them that he hails from one of their *major* prospects. Suddenly, his boss's look of shock turns to one of admiration and approval. *Why didn't he say so from the beginning? If Toby could make a sale like that, the whole company could benefit.*

The boss gives Toby's friend a firm handshake and tells him it's an absolute pleasure to meet him. Toby explains that they were just having lunch at the clubhouse restaurant when his "client" suggested playing a few holes. "I'm sorry. I should have called to let you know I'd be out longer," Toby tells his boss.

"Absolutely no need to apologize. You take as long as you want." Toby has not only bypassed getting caught, but he's managed to make a great impression on his boss *and* the CEO of the company.

"Keep an eye on that one," the CEO says to Toby's boss as he pulls two cigars from his jacket. "He's going places." The CEO hands Toby's boss a stogy and lights his own. Toby walks back to his game to finish the hole with an air of confidence. Toby's game may not improve much today, but his boss's perspective of him sure does.

WORK BULLSHIT: Bullshitting Your Coworkers

The Christmas party couldn't have come any sooner. This is the first time in the past few months that anyone in the office has had the chance to breathe and let loose, and everyone is making sure to take full advantage of it (spiked eggnog doesn't hurt, either).

Charlie started working here three weeks ago, right in the thick of it. Small talk was nonexistent and tensions were high. *Extremely high.* He likened those first three weeks to stepping onto the New York Stock Exchange at the exact moment when every stock plummeted. But the office he is seeing now is something altogether different. Laughter has replaced screaming and the frantic running has switched to relaxed groups with drinks in hand.

This is Charlie's chance to shine. If he had tried being Mr. Likable during that hectic time, he would have come across as completely unprofessional, a nuisance, and left everyone wondering why he was even hired in the first place. But this party is the perfect opportunity to unleash his bullshit.

The agenda of today's BS is not about making new friends. This is about establishing contacts, networks, and making sure he is on the good side of the people who can help him succeed.

The office grows quiet as the ring of tapping a glass slowly permeates the room. "Excuse me, everybody. If I could just have your attention for a few seconds." Charlie stops tapping his wine glass and sets it on the counter. His bullshit is about to begin—and boy, is he ready.

"I know I haven't been here long, but I just wanted to say that watching you all work so hard these past few weeks has been an awe-inspiring and humbling experience. I haven't had the opportunity to meet all of you yet, and I'd like to do just that. So after this party, you're all invited back to my place for drinks."

Charlie has established his charm and likeability. Off to a very good start.

When the cheers and applause die down, Charlie carries on with part two of his plan. He approaches the stronger coworkers of the company. *These were the people from whom he could gain the most.* Now that they are aware of who Charlie is, they welcome him with open arms.

As the conversation progresses, it somehow turns to politics. Charlie has gotten a feel for the political tone of these gentlemen early on, and begins advocating these same beliefs. (In all reality, he doesn't share a single belief of any of these men. But he isn't going to let *them* know that.)

Eventually, Charlie moves the conversation along to new topics. One, in particular, is how difficult it is for a new guy to build relationships with clients.

Suddenly, one of his coworkers stops him and says, "Look, I wouldn't do this for anybody, but I can already tell you're a good guy. I've got someone that I'd be willing to give you." Charlie is taken aback. "No, I wouldn't want you to do that. That's your client!"

"Please," his coworker insists, "This guy has given me consistent work for four years. If I say I like somebody, he'll work with them."

The rest of Charlie's night unfolds in a similar fashion. It doesn't matter if it is politics, sports, arts, or history, Charlie seeks to make those connections, regardless of whether he authentically agrees with a position. By the time the party moves to his place that night, he has made enough contacts to last him well into the New Year. Maybe it is the holiday spirit and the gift of giving that makes everyone so generous, or maybe it is because he is one great bullshitter. (Hint: It's the latter.)

WORK BULLSHIT: Bullshitting Coworkers and Your Boss—at the Same Time

Stephanie's boss puts a massively important assignment on her plate. Always the multitasker and wanting to look good in front of her boss, she takes it on, even though she's already working on another project. Stephanie sees her coworker Lisa at the copy machine. Despite the fact that they started the same day and came in with relatively the same amount of knowledge and experience, Stephanie has double—if not triple—the workload of Lisa. And there's a very simple reason for this. Stephanie is in no way a better worker than Lisa, but right from the beginning, she made sure she got to know her boss on a personal level.

It started when she saw a picture on her boss's desk. It was a picture of him and his wife standing on a boat. He had a huge, proud smile on his face, and as you followed his eyes down, they led to a monstrous fish, its mouth still attached to the fishing line. Immediately, Stephanie started researching all there was to know on the subject.

She put that knowledge to good use. One day, Stephanie was talking to a coworker and her boss was nearby. Somehow Stephanie got on the subject of fishing (not coincidentally, mind you), and how much she enjoyed it. Her boss's head seem to perk up and he walked over to Stephanie and asked, "You fish?"

Stephanie went on about her love of fishing and how every summer she goes to her lake house (which she doesn't have). "Two years ago, I caught my all-time record, a six-pound walleye." (The walleye is, of course, native to the particular area of her lake house.)

Ever since that conversation, her boss, whom most would say isn't a very likable guy, has become friendly with Stephanie. He likes what he sees in her, and between fishing tales, he hands her assignments meant for people in much higher positions than hers.

Meanwhile, Lisa is still photocopying and scanning her days away. She made no real attempt to connect with the boss. She figures if the work is satisfactory, that should be enough. Unfortunately, her logic is flawed, and she is never handed any work that would allow her to prove herself.

Stephanie doesn't gloat about her success. She knows better than that. When she sees Lisa by the copying machine, she knows exactly how to solve her workload problem. There is no feasible way Stephanie can complete all of these assignments, but she can't let her boss know that. She's worked too hard for this and showing any sign of weakness would be detrimental to her growth within the company.

Stephanie knows Lisa is looking for a chance to prove herself. "I know you want bigger projects, and I've got just the thing."

Stephanie tells Lisa about the other, nonpriority assignment she has in her queue. "This thing is top priority and needs to get done ASAP. I'll be working on the second part of it, and they need to go together, so just hand it to me when you're finished."

At around 4:45 P.M., Stephanie enters her boss's office. She hands him the first assignment. His face says it all. *Atta' girl. Nicely done*. But Stephanie is not finished. She then hands him the second project (which Lisa completed). "Oh, and I finished this one too."

"You finished both of these in one day? Jesus, how'd you manage that?" Stephanie stands there and smiles. She had learned one thing from all this bullshitting on fishing: throw in the bait, wait for the fish to bite, and then reel it in. "I'm just a hard worker, I guess."

SOCIAL BULLSHIT: Bullshitting the Opposite Sex at a Bar

Jake sees a beautiful woman at the other end of the bar. Judging by the number of guys around her offering to buy her drinks, Jake knows this is going to be a tough one. Jake watches for a little while, taking in all he can about this mystery girl. When finally he feels he has enough information on how to tackle the situation, he goes to the bar.

As he squeezes through the horde of men, he finally reaches the woman and hands her one of two drinks that he had been holding. "Um, what's this?" she asks him, knowing better than to take a drink from a total stranger. "Water," he says, smiling. "I figured with all of these guys giving you booze you might need some." She is taken aback for a moment. She smiles at him and takes a small sip. Once positive that it is, in fact, water, her smile grows wider. Extending her hand, she says, "I'm Claire." His opener worked. Now he just has to make sure he doesn't lose her interest, which shouldn't be too hard.

Jake takes her hand and leans in, whispering, "Shiva, right?" Jake motions at Claire's neck, where she has a small tattoo of a human figure sitting. Claire's entire face brightens up. Her eyes open widely and she puts one hand on Jake and the other on her tattoo. "Not too many people know what that is." She smiles at Jake. Jake introduces himself and Claire asks, "How long have you been doing yoga?"

"I've just started taking classes." Not only had Jake never taken a yoga class, but he could barely touch his toes. He knew absolutely nothing about the subject prior to doing some preliminary research on his cell phone moments before.

But Jake was smart about his bullshit. He knew that he couldn't just flat out say he was an expert in yoga. Never having actually done a downward dog, if asked to do one, he'd come up panting (looking more like a thirsty dog). At this point, however, it no longer matters. Jake has already distinguished himself from the other men crowded around Claire. They have a shared interest (or so she thinks), and she is enjoying his company. From here, their conversation could go anywhere. And hey, with him being a novice and all, maybe she could give him some pointers at his place later that night. . . .

SOCIAL BULLSHIT: Bullshitting to Be Popular

Peter enters the house knowing one person—the guy who brought him there (and even that is a stretch). Being new in town meant friends and acquaintances are few and far between. When his neighbor knocks on the door and asks if he wants to go to a party instead of the alternative (spending a Saturday night unpacking more boxes), Peter jumps at the opportunity.

He has never been one of the "popular guys," so this is his chance for a fresh start. Usually more reserved and quiet, Peter is excited about the party. This is Peter's chance to show off his bullshitting chops.

On the drive over, Peter is given the lowdown on some of the people who will be there that night. "Alice is throwing the thing. She just got back from Sweden," his neighbor begins to say. "She was over there for work and this is the first time any of us have seen her since she left four months ago. Her brother, Nick, he'll probably be there, too. He's finishing up art school now—a sculpture major." The drive continues like this. Peter listens intently as his neighbor goes into great detail about some of the usual crew.

The music is loud and the place smells like stale beer. There are people everywhere—exactly what Peter wanted to see. Before even being introduced, Peter can tell who the key players are. He judges Alice is the woman on the couch showing everyone pictures. That seems pretty obvious. There is a scrawnier guy in the back with dyed hair—Nick, he presumes. Peter scans the room, trying to pin down each person according to his neighbor's description.

As he speaks to them, it is as if Peter is an expert on the very subject that interests each person. He speaks to Nick about sculptures by Henry Moore and he converses with Alice about Sweden's current political affairs (all of which he had only researched moments before). He speaks about what it was like when he went to Europe (which he has never done) and compares it to Alice's four months abroad. He is charming, he is attentive, he is engaging, and everything that comes out of his mouth is bullshit.

The guy who once was the staple wallflower at parties is now being dragged from end to end like some toy everyone wants to show. "Oh, you have to meet Stacy. You'd love her." "Have you met Helen yet? I think you two would have a lot to talk about." Peter is certain they will have a lot to talk about, no matter what the subject is.

SOCIAL BULLSHIT: Bullshitting Through a Family Function

Adam is spending Thanksgiving with his girlfriend's family this year. He enjoys spending time with her parents on their own, but when the whole family is there, the night just turns into one giant conversation revolving around sports. Adam, a graphic designer by trade, always considers himself more of the artsy type and never really *gets* sports. It just isn't his thing—a big attraction for his girlfriend when they began dating. He was so different from everything she grew up around and she found it refreshing.

Now, however, she is beginning to see his lack of interest as a handicap. The last time her whole family got together, the conversation quickly turned to sports and Adam remained quiet for much of the night. His girlfriend is starting to worry that Adam won't be able to connect with her family, and family has always been extremely important to her.

This Thanksgiving, however, Adam is a completely different person. His girlfriend's brothers are talking to him about teams and statistics, and Adam is not only engaged in the conversation, but he's actually leading it. What happened? Did Adam suddenly take an interest in sports? Did he start watching games?

Not a chance. Before arriving, Adam looked up three facts about a team's star player, and read a newspaper article about how the team was doing this season. Using this information, Adam throws one or two points out and lets the conversation progress. By the time he runs out of information, it doesn't matter. His stance is firm, and he can now bullshit his way through the rest of the night by focusing on the bigger picture ideas. Even better for Adam, though, is now that he feels comfortable talking, he can steer the conversation away from sports without it seeming obvious.

If the conversation returns to sports, Adam need not worry, because everyone there already knows his take on the subject. All he has to do is get the right information, and he can use the family's knowledge to supplement his viewpoint. Adam manages to bullshit his girlfriend's family for the entire Thanksgiving meal. Now that's a reason to give thanks.

OTHER BULLSHIT: Bullshitting to Get Out of a Commitment

It should be a crime to have a child's birthday party on Super Bowl Sunday. Andrew chalks it up to one thing and one thing only, "God must hate me. I don't know what I've done, but I've done something very wrong."

While Andrew sulks about the desperate situation, his wife is in panic mode. She is already running late and has forgotten to get a present. How could she forget a present for her own brother's child? And just like that, Andrew's faith is restored.

"I'll go buy a gift. You leave now, and I'll run to the store and get something."

As his wife says, "Thank you for being such a great husband," all Andrew can think is, *Thank you for being so forgetful.* But he sounds more like, "Of course. I should leave soon though. I would hate to get to the party too late."

And late he is. Keeping his wife updated with phone calls and text messages (U WUD NOT BELIEVE THE TRAFFIC! :(, TOY STORE IN MALL CLOSED DOWN??, NEVR SEEN SUCH LONGLINES AT THIS STORE b4!), Andrew manages to watch the majority of the game at a local sports bar. By the time the fourth quarter rolls around, there is no point in staying. His team has lost. His bullshit, however, has won big time.

When he finally does make it to the party, he looks like a hero. "I can't believe all the trouble you went through. Thank you so much, honey."

"Of course," Andrew says to his wife, "I'm just bummed I missed so much of the party."

OTHER BULLSHIT: Bullshitting to Get Something You Want

Brian stares at the 72-inch screen with a smile that reflects back at him from the glossy surface. This isn't a question of want; he *needs* to have this television. He will not go home without it. Of course, his wife might feel otherwise.

"This is a one-of-a-kind deal. There isn't a better price around and it's going to be gone tomorrow if we don't get it now. I've read all about it online. The one we've got will be obsolete in two years, tops. But this thing is state of the art and has all the latest technology." Brian isn't whining or begging to his wife, simply stating the facts (even if they aren't necessarily "facts" per se). He goes into great detail about the specs and how the television they own now will be "rendered useless" as he puts it. Of course, none of it is true, but he makes it seem like this television was built by NASA, and the one they currently own is more like a horse and buggy with one of its wheels missing.

"And you've always wanted to host more functions. Think about how great it will be for Dylan and Eric to invite their friends over for movie nights. We could make it a weekly thing. They'd think they have the cool parents and we won't have to worry about their getting into any trouble." Those are buzzwords for her, all right. Chosen and executed to perfection.

Brian speaks with so much enthusiasm about the television that his wife even starts to feel enthusiastic about it. And that's when Brian starts to tone it down. He shrugs and begins to pull her away. "Maybe we'll get one next year."

As Brian starts to walk away, his wife stops him dead in his tracks. "I think we should get it."

As they wait in the checkout line, a salesperson that has been watching the whole time calls Brian to the side. He looks at Brian and says, "Do you want a job? Because that was some of the best selling I've ever seen."

SAMPLE QUESTIONS:
1. What is Work Bullshit?
2. What are the main goals involved in WBS?
3. What is Social Bullshit?
4. What are the main goals involved in SBS?
5. What is Other Bullshit?
6. What are the main goals involved in OBS?
7. What are the main differences among the three?

QUESTIONS TO ASK YOURSELF:
- How can you use bullshit at your job?
- How can you use bullshit to enhance your social life?
- Is there anything that you want? How can you use bullshit to get it?
- Should I look into starting a yoga class?

Now that you've got the who, what, where, when, why, and how covered, you've almost got what it takes to become a true Bullshit Artist. *Almost.* There's still one thing left to know. . . .

Chapter 5

When the Bullshit Hits the Fan

"I wouldn't give myself any advice, because advice is kinda bullshit. Take a deep breath and don't take any of it too seriously."

—CHER

Bullshit is—and always will be—a game of trial and error. It's never a guaranteed thing, and when you're caught lying, it can turn ugly really fast. To be a true Bullshit Artist, you need to learn from those moments when you get called out and work through them as they unfold. Eventually, you'll get a handle on how far your abilities can take you and you'll know how and when to push your BS further.

Being a Bullshit Artist doesn't mean you won't have off days, but it does mean you know how to handle your failure and pick yourself up when you do. Every bullshitter's nightmare is getting called out on his or her BS. Unfortunately, even the best bullshitters screw up every now and then, and you will be no different.

Spewing Shit is a natural part of the Bullshit Artist's process.

Spewed Shit is unavoidable and a necessary evil. Why? Well, think of it this way. A professional baseball player doesn't hit a homer every time he's at bat. Sometimes it's a swing and a miss. Hell, even when he hits the ball, it's not a guaranteed home run. The ball can go far and high, it can slide to the ground, it can turn into a foul play—and he can be out before he even makes it to first base. The point of bullshitting isn't about hitting the ball out of the park every time; it's about playing the game for all nine innings and coming out the winner.

Spewed Shit puts you in your place. It humbles you. It is the best way to learn the dos and don'ts of bullshitting. That way, you won't repeat the same mistake twice. And if you do, at least you'll have a better understanding of how to handle it the next time.

You know what they say about falling off a horse? You get right back on. Bullshit is no different. If you fall off that mechanical bull(shit), get right back on and hold on for dear life for as long as you can. Don't get discouraged after a failure and don't let it shake you. You control the bullshit, not the other way around.

HISTORICAL MOMENT OF SPEWED SHIT
THE NIXON INTERVIEWS WITH DAVID FROST, 1977
Some shit spewers never learn. After failing to bullshit his way out of the Watergate scandal and resigning from the presidency, Richard Nixon agreed to sit down for a series of interviews with a young British journalist by the name of David Frost. When Frost questioned Nixon about the legality of his cover-up, Nixon was his usual Spewed Shit self.

WHAT HE SAID: "Well, when the president does it, that means that it is not illegal."
WHAT HE SHOULD HAVE SAID: Anything else. Jesus Christ, seriously, *anything* else.

If you are still deep into your bullshit and sense something is wrong, do everything in your ability to adjust. Remember what you've learned from your exercises and try to bullshit the person in a different way. If your bullshit starts to turn sour to the point of no return, don't just drop everything and leave in the middle of the conversation.

Some people believe the best way to redeem yourself when caught in a lie is to fess up and admit what you've done—then apologize. And to the supporters and followers of this philosophy, I say: bullshit!

It is absolutely possible to recover from being called out without fessing up to your lie, but it takes practice and it's not easy.

How to Rebound When You're Called Out on Your Bullshit

You can all tell when the tide starts to turn. Maybe your voice gives you away, maybe you start to fidget more, maybe the other person starts to break eye contact, or maybe the other person has actual physical evidence that proves you're lying (ouch). When your lie is discovered, it's the big elephant in the room that you just want to tranquilize and remove from the premises as quickly as possible. And elephants are heavy and stubborn. They won't go without a fight. (An adult male elephant is also called a bull. Coincidence? I think no—actually, yeah. It's just a coincidence.)

If you want to make it through the situation in one piece with your reputation intact, you must remain completely calm. You can't come off like a deer in headlights (what's with all of the animal references?)....your body language will show the first indications that something is going wrong and you must be able to control that. Excellent bullshit is all about mind over matter. Remember, unchecked body language can tip a person off before you even have a chance to say anything. If you get called out, whatever you do, do not panic.

Your next move is critical. Once you've composed yourself, start thinking—and start thinking quickly. The downside to getting caught in your lie (besides the obvious failure to reach your goal) is that your target loses trust in you. And once you've lost the trust, it can be tough to regain it. You need to use your training to get back on track. Getting caught in a lie can be a slippery slope and at the bottom you'll be belly flopping into a pool of Spewed Shit. Avoiding the pool puts the true Bullshit Artist to the test.

So what do you do? There are several steps you can take depending on the severity of the situation.

If you haven't been caught yet, either try changing the subject *subtly*, or fix and tweak your bullshit. Another great way to circumvent Spewed Shit is to chalk it up to a simple misunderstanding. Make sure that once you "understand" what you are supposed to be talking about, you're saying the right thing and you do a good job covering yourself.

If you're caught red-handed—we're talking no way out—the absolute worst thing you can do is deny your lie. But didn't I just say you don't have to fess up? Well, you don't. Are you confused? Don't be.

Do admit that you were lying. If you get caught and it's obvious, there really isn't much else you can do about it. You might try to claim a misunderstanding, but if you're in deep enough, that will just sound like Spewed Shit. No, you need to come clean . . . ish.

Honesty is the best policy . . . to fake.

Just because you were caught lying doesn't mean you have to tell the truth. Admitting you were lying and admitting the truth are two very different things. Admit you were lying, sure. It's the only option. But under no circumstance should you tell the other person the true reason as to why you were lying. Never let her know your true intent. Adjust your bullshit antennas, make sure you have a clear picture, and start the bullshitting process all over again.

For this to work, you've got to be believable. Not only should you sound sincere and apologetic, but more importantly, you should sound like you are the good guy in all of this. Whatever you do, don't let your audience in on the fact that you lied to get your way. Instead, make it seem like you lied so as not to hurt the other person's feelings. Or tell them you lied because something else has been worrying you and you didn't feel comfortable enough to talk about it.

Your bullshit will transform, yes, and you will have to make the proper adjustments, but you won't be found out. You can still bullshit the other person and work towards getting what you want. That's what makes you a real Bullshit Artist.

The Importance of Knowing Something Before Saying Anything

As I've said, it's always best to do research before going into your bullshitting situation (if you can). Bullshitting on the fly is much harder and leaves more room for mistakes.

If you place a select few kernels of truth into your bullshit, you'll be able to cook up a mean batch of popcorn and everybody will eat it. Hard facts ground your bullshit. You're no longer talking about big thoughts and ideas that can be questioned or confronted by the other person. Incorporating real information into your BS validates what you have to say and makes it seem grounded. Once the other person buys into it, you'll be able to take your bullshit to new heights.

Incorporating information, by itself, is a test on your abilities as a Bullshit Artist. The trick is not to overwhelm the other person with facts and information. Like everything else, you want the material to seem natural. This isn't a lightning round in some sort of game show. You need to weave this information into conversation so it appears natural and believable.

So where are you supposed to get these facts? Well, you can spend your life reading every newspaper, textbook, encyclopedia, magazine, novel, and tabloid in existence while simultaneously playing National Public Radio 24/7—or, you know, you can turn to Part 2 of this book. The choice is yours, really. Here's your last quiz. Thank God, right?

SAMPLE QUESTIONS:
1. You have been called out on your bullshit. Should you:
   A. Fess up that you've been lying the whole time.
   B. Ignore it.
   C. Admit that you were lying but provide another lie in its place as the reason why.
   D. Walk away.
2. Why is remaining calm so important if you are called out on your BS?
3. Why is it important to have some knowledge of a topic before bullshitting?

ANSWER:

1. A

QUESTIONS TO ASK YOURSELF:
- What signs do I notice when my bullshit is being detected?
- What can I do to fix my bullshit before it's too late?
- Do I usually go into a scenario with my bullshit already planned out or do I improvise?
- What am I still doing on this page when there's a whole second half of this book to read?

The first part of this book focused on the training of a Bullshit Artist. Now that you're trained in how to bullshit, it's time to learn little tidbits of information to enhance your art. With bullshit, the world can be your oyster. So turn the page, learn the information, and get shucking.

"That director is truly one of today's true auteurs, wouldn't you say?"

"I haven't seen a witch hunt like this since McCarthy's HUAC hearings."

"When it comes to geological time periods, I've always been quite partial to the Phanerozoic Eon, myself."

PART 2

THE SCIENCE OF BULLSHITTING—OR, USEFUL SHIT

"I think it's clear to see that if we were to apply the Socratic method we would get better and faster results."

"What a coincidence! I can't believe someone else here likes German Expressionist architecture as much as I do!"

Chapter 6

Religion— God Looks the Other Way

JUDAISM

Choosing the right things to say for the chosen people.

THE BELIEFS

- There is one God who is omnipotent and omniscient.
- The Torah (Old Testament) is the primary source of religious doctrine. It contains the Ten Commandments.
- Moses was the greatest prophet.
- The Messiah hasn't come yet.

THE MAJOR HOLIDAYS

- Rosh Hashanah is the Jewish New Year.
- Yom Kippur is a day to repent for one's sins. Jewish people will fast and deprive themselves of pleasure until it gets dark, when they break the fast with a feast.
- Passover is an eight-day celebration commemorating when Moses led the Jewish people out of Egypt, where they had been enslaved by the Pharaoh.

- Chanukah is the Festival of Lights celebrating the rededication of the Holy Temple in Jerusalem.
- Purim is a festival commemorating the salvation of the Jews from a massacre plotted by Haman, a Persian nobleman.

THE INTERESTING FACTS

- Judaism was one of the original monotheistic religions to appear at a time where most religions were polytheistic.
- In 1965, Sandy Koufax, pitcher for the Los Angeles Dodgers, skipped Game One of the World Series because it was Yom Kippur.
- Non-Jews are referred to as "Gentiles."

WHEN TO BULLSHIT
- When attending a Jewish holiday.
- When attending a Bar or Bat Mitzvah.
- When trying to woo a Jewish girl or guy.
- When trying to get back the money you lost in a game of dreidel.

CHRISTIANITY
The Old Testament gets an addition . . . and a Messiah.

THE BELIEFS
- There is one God.
- The Holy Trinity, God, exists as the Father, the Son, and the Holy Spirit.
- The Bible is made up of the Old Testament (the Hebrew portion) and the New Testament (the books about Jesus).
- Jesus was crucified and killed for the sins of the people, and resurrected from the dead the following Sunday.
- Jesus will return to judge the living and the dead.
- Jesus will save all those who believe in him, and condemn those who don't to hell.

ABOUT JESUS CHRIST

- Jesus Christ is the Messiah, the Son of God.
- Jesus, a Jew born in Bethlehem and living in Nazareth, was immaculately conceived, lived a life free of sin, performed miracles, was crucified for his teachings, and resurrected from his death.
- His mother was the Virgin Mary, and Joseph, a carpenter, was considered his stepfather.
- The only way to repent for one's sins is to accept Jesus Christ as the Lord and Savior.

MIRACLES OF CHRIST

- Changing water into wine.
- Healing the sick.
- Walking on water.
- Healing the blind man, the paralyzed man, and a man with dropsy.

CATHOLICISM, PROTESTANTISM, AND EASTERN ORTHODOXY

- Though all three are considered Christian faiths, there are some key differences, such as papal authority, and the roles of saints and scriptures.

WHEN TO BULLSHIT

- When attending a holiday party, Baptism, or church service.
- When you are the only Jew surrounded by Gentiles, you'll have something to talk about.

ISLAM

Building on Judaism and Christianity, a new prophet and a new faith.

THE BELIEFS

- There is one God, and unlike Christianity, there is no Trinity.
- Angels exist.
- Islam believes in the prophets found in the Old and New Testament; however, the final prophet was Muhammad.

- The latest scripture, the Quran, was revealed to Muhammad.
- The Day of Judgment is when all people will be resurrected and judged by God.
- Predestination is the notion that God knows all, and even though humans have free will, God knows the choices they will make.

THE FIVE PILLARS
- The duties Muslims perform to demonstrate their faith.
  1. Testimony of Faith—one must say, "There is no God, but Allah, and Muhammad is the Prophet of Allah."
  2. Prayer—a Muslim must pray five times a day facing the direction of Mecca.
  3. *Zakat* (Giving to the Needy)—if a person can afford to, they must give a fixed percentage of wealth to those in need.
  4. Fasting during Ramadan—Muslims are to fast for the entire month of the holiday from sunrise to sunset. (Dates change every year according to the Islamic lunar calendar.)
  5. Pilgrimage to Mecca—hajj is an annual journey to Mecca, which every able Muslim person must make.

WHEN TO BULLSHIT
- When traveling to the Middle East.
- When discussing world affairs (to avoid sounding ignorant).

BUDDHISM
Reaching Nirvana.

THE BELIEFS
- The Emphasis is on seeing truth and reaching enlightenment.
- Religion is based on the teachings of the Buddha, or awakened one.
- Upon dying, a person is reincarnated, or reborn, and can go through many cycles of birth, life, death, and rebirth until one reaches Nirvana, the extreme state where one is free from suffering.
- Happiness is attainable to everyone through meditation.

THE FOUR NOBLE TRUTHS

1. In life there is suffering.
2. There is a cause for the suffering.
3. Suffering can end.
4. There is a path (the Eightfold Path) to end suffering and bring one to enlightenment.

THE EIGHTFOLD PATH

1. Understanding the Four Noble Truths. (Wisdom)
2. Having the right thinking. (Wisdom)
3. Having the right speech (not lying and being kind). (Morality)
4. Having the right conduct. (Morality)
5. Having the right livelihood and not hurting others to support yourself. (Morality)
6. Promoting good thoughts and getting rid of evil thoughts. (Meditation)
7. Becoming aware of your feelings, mind, and body. (Meditation)
8. Achieving a higher level of consciousness through meditation. (Meditation)

INFORMATION TO USE WHEN BULLSHITTING

- Buddhism is the only major religion that doesn't worship a divine being.

WHEN TO BULLSHIT

- When trying to convince someone you don't need therapy because you have found inner peace.
- The next time you order Buddha's Delight at a Chinese restaurant, you can question whether this would actually delight Buddha.

HINDU

One God, many forms.

THE BELIEFS

- The majority of Hindus are henotheistic, meaning they believe in one deity, but it manifests as many different forms of gods and goddesses.

- Some view God as a triad
  1. Brahma, the creator
  2. Vishnu, the preserver
  3. Shiva, the destroyer

SACRED TEXTS

- The Vedas are the sacred text of the Hindu people. Each Veda has rituals, prayers, and hymns from ancient India.
- There are four Vedas
  1. *Rig* Veda
  2. *Sama* Veda
  3. *Yajur* Veda
  4. *Atharva* Veda
- The Ramayana is an epic poem following Rama, an avatar of Vishnu and also a deity on his own. It teaches about dharma, or the righteous duty of a person.
- The Mahabharata is a group of books telling the legends of one of the Aryan tribal groups.

THE FOUR AIMS OF HINDUISM

- Dharma—righteousness in religion
- Artha—financial success
- Kama—gratifying the senses such as sexual, sensual, and mental
- Moksa—liberating from samsara, the cycle of birth, life, death, and rebirth

WHEN TO BULLSHIT

- When traveling to India.
- When trying to sound cultured and open-minded as you take a date out for Indian food.

SIKHISM

Liberating the spirit and removing social injustices.

THE BELIEFS

- There is one formless God that can be known through meditation.
- The God of Sikhism is represented by a symbol, and is referred to as Ik Onkar.
- Sikhism forbids the worship of idols or images.
- Sikhism rejects the Hindu caste system, believing everyone to be equal in the eyes of God regardless of race, religion, or sex.
- Similar to Hindu, Sikhs believe in samsara (reincarnation) and karma.
- Sikhism places importance on earning an honest living and sharing with those in need.

THE ORIGINS

- Sikhism was founded by Guru Nanak, who criticized the teachings of Islam and Hinduism.
- Nanak passed his wisdom on to nine other Gurus, the last one being Gobind Singh, who would go on to create the Khalsa order, men and women who uphold the highest virtues of Sikhism.

THE HOLY TEXT

- The Sri Guru Granth Sahib is the holy text of Sikhism; it includes the teachings of the Ten Sikh Gurus.

INFORMATION TO USE WHEN BULLSHITTING

- Estimates are that Sikhism is the fifth largest religion in the world.
- Many consider the Golden Temple in the state of Punjab as the most significant religious center.

WHEN TO BULLSHIT

- When interacting with a Sikh so you don't seem clueless.

JAINISM
Equal respect all around.

THE BELIEFS
- Jains share some of the beliefs of Hinduism and Buddhism.
- The religion is based on the teachings of Mahavira found in the sacred texts, the Agamas.
- There is no deity in Jainism.
- Jains believe humans, animals, and plants all have living souls of equal value, and deserve equal respect.
- Jains are strict vegetarians.
- Jains believe in reincarnation, karma, and moksha (end to the reincarnation cycle).

THE THREE JEWELS
- The right faith—seeing things clearly
- The right knowledge—being free from desire and attachment
- The right behavior—avoid harming others and freeing yourself from impure thoughts and actions

THE FIVE PRINCIPLES OF LIVING
1. *Ahimsa*—avoiding violence mentally, verbally, and physically
2. *Satya*—speaking the truth
3. *Asteya*—do not steal
4. *Brahmacharya*—being sexually committed to only one's spouse
5. *Aparigraha*—abstaining from excessive material possessions and overindulging.

WHEN TO BULLSHIT
- When making conversation with a vegetarian.
- When trying to get out of a hunting trip.
- When trying to explain why you're so cheap (use *Aparigraha*).

WICCA
Pagans, witches, and sex, oh my!

THE BELIEFS
- The largest Neo-Pagan religion, Wicca is based on pre-Christian religion found in Scotland, Wales, and Ireland.
- Wiccans can be monotheist, polytheist, or atheist, but many believe in a Horned God representing wilderness, nature, sexuality, and hunting, and a Triple Goddess, representing wisdom, fertility, and virginity.
- Wiccans have a high respect for nature and believe that everything has a spirit, including plants, animals, and stars.
- Females are respected equally, and Wiccans believe the natural world has a sexual polarity, with parts of nature representing the male and other parts representing the female.
- Sexuality is embraced and considered a gift from the God or Goddess.
- Thoughts about what happens after death vary, with ideas ranging from reincarnation to the body's molecules dispersing into other living beings. Some believe there is nothing after death.

WITCHCRAFT
- Wicca is a form of witchcraft.
- Wiccans practice white magic, which is good magic, and protection magic to ward off evil spirits and energies.
- The Wiccan Rede is a code of conduct for all witches (Wiccans).

WHEN TO BULLSHIT
- Instead of being a swinger, just tell people you're a Wiccan and you're embracing your God-given gift.

SCIENTOLOGY
A self-help guide from a sci-fi guy.

THE ORIGINS
- Created by science fiction writer L. Ron Hubbard, scientology means the study of knowledge or truth.
- Hubbard originally wrote a self-help book called *Dianetics: The Modern Science of Mental Health*, which became the precursor to Scientology.

THE BELIEFS
- A person is divided into three parts
  - Body—including the brain, with its main purpose of carrying messages.
  - Mind—accumulation of experiences, perceptions, memories, and decisions.
  - Thetan—the soul of a person.
- An Operating Thetan practices exteriorization, where the thetan can leave the body but still maintain control over it. This brings a new state of awareness and enlightenment.
- After the death of one body, the thetan takes on a new body in an endless cycle.
- Thetans in their "native states" are godlike, with the potential of knowing all, but that information has been lost or forgotten over time.
- Through a process called auditing, people free themselves of the material world to reach a heightened state.

CONTROVERSY
- Scientology has very strict copyright regulations covering its texts and symbols, and there is a disconnection policy where members are instructed to cut off those who have strayed from Scientology.

WHEN TO BULLSHIT
- When discussing New Age religions.
- When mingling with celebrities.

ATHEISM

There is no God.

THE BELIEFS
- Atheism is not a religion in the ways Judaism, Christianity, and Islam are.
- There are no moral codes, religious texts, or holidays.
- Atheists reject the notion of any deities or higher beings such as a God and believe the existence of a higher being is impossible.
- Atheists believe there is no evidence to prove the existence of a higher power and life evolved on this earth through natural selection.
- Atheism differs from agnosticism because it clearly states that God does not exist and leaves no possibility of the existence of a higher power.

IMPLICIT ATHEISM
- Implicit atheism is the unconscious rejection of the belief in a higher being.
- An implicit atheist has never been introduced to the concept of a higher power, and therefore does not believe in it.
  - Example: Newborn babies are born with no belief in any sort of deity. They are too young to comprehend or know what God is and are only introduced to the notion at a later time in their lives.

EXPLICIT ATHEISM
- Explicit atheism is the conscious rejection in the belief of a higher being.
  - Example: A person claims that the existence of God is impossible, irrational, and, further, that they do not believe in any form of higher power.

WHEN TO BULLSHIT
- When caught in a religious debate.
- When trying to get out of going to church or temple.
- When telling someone why you don't want to drive through the Bible Belt.

Chapter 7

Art—Because a Painting Is Never *Just* a Painting

ANCIENT GREEK

Making art more human since 750 B.C.

WHAT IT WAS

- The art of ancient Greece placed great attention on mimicking nature (known as mimesis) and understanding the human figure.

ARCHAIC ART (750–500 B.C.)

- Art of this time was heavily influenced by the large sculptures of Egypt, and focused on accurately portraying the human figure, steering away from geometric patterning.
- Sculptures were used for government and religious purposes.
- The most dominant sculptures were the front-facing kouros (male) and kore (female) statues that stood straight in very rigid poses, and were carved out of marble.

CLASSICAL ART (480–338 B.C.)

- The poses of statues were no longer static, instead showing expression, emphasizing movement and naturalism.
- Human figures became freestanding and were sculpted in stone and bronze.
- Statues portrayed gods as the perfect human.
- This era is the first time individual sculptors become known for their work.

HELLENISTIC ART (338–31 B.C.)

- Art shifted away from religion and more toward naturalism, realism, and human psychology.
- Poses became more dramatic and theatrical, playing with light and shade, and including the statue's physical surroundings.
- Instead of the idea of the perfect human, emphasis was put on everyday people and their imperfections, including expressions of pain and despair.

WHEN TO BULLSHIT
- When discussing art history with someone.
- When talking with someone over a glass of the traditional Greek drink, ouzo.

BYZANTINE

Classical art meets Christianity.
WHEN: (A.D. 330–1453)

ABOUT THE BYZANTINE EMPIRE

- Originally, it was the eastern part of the Roman Empire; Constantine (the first Christian emperor) relocated the capital to Byzantium and named it Constantinople.
- When the Roman Empire fell, the Eastern Roman Empire continued to flourish. Over time, it would become known as the Byzantine Empire.
- The Byzantine Empire would thrive for 1,000 years after the fall of Rome.

THE ARTWORK

- Artwork of the Byzantine Empire was greatly influenced by the art of ancient Greece and incorporated many of its themes.
- The humanism found in ancient Greek art was now replaced with the ideals of Orthodox Christianity.
- Byzantine art focused solely on religion and less attention was spent on realism.
- Byzantine art introduced iconography and symbols to painting.
- Paintings were more flat and simplified, featuring outlines with no emphasis, shadow, or dimension.
- Paintings no longer depicted nudes or such intense study of the human figure.
- Typically, those depicted in paintings were God, Jesus, the Virgin Mary, and the martyrs and the saints.

WHEN TO BULLSHIT

- When stuck in a room of art history buffs.
- When trying to impress a date at the museum.

RENAISSANCE

Remember Classicism? They did.

WHAT IT WAS

- Breaking away from Byzantine art and the Middle Ages, the Renaissance marks the rebirth of ancient Greek principles.

EARLY RENAISSANCE (A.D.1330–1450)

- Artists believed classic Greek and Roman artwork set the standard, and artwork focused once again on humanism and naturalism.
- Christian figures were portrayed realistically instead of stylized, with emphasis placed on showing real emotions and correct proportions.
- To attain more realism, artists began incorporating depth of field, linear perspective, and new methods of shading.

- Example of artwork—Donatello's *David*, a bronze statue depicting the naked youth standing over the head of Goliath. The figure stands in a Greek pose and shows the beginning of naturalist ideas.

HIGH RENAISSANCE (1490–1530)
- The techniques that were started in the Early Renaissance were mastered by artists of the High Renaissance.
- High Renaissance artists include Leonardo da Vinci, Michelangelo, and Raphael.
- Example of artwork—Michelangelo's *David*. Standing at 13 feet tall, the statue depicts David as a well-defined, muscular man, preparing to go into battle. The figure stands in a very pronounced Greek pose.

NORTHERN RENAISSANCE (1500–1600)
- Principles of the Italian Renaissance spread throughout Europe.
- Paintings of the Northern Renaissance shifted away from religion, and presented everyday scenes with common people.
- Example of artwork—Jan Van Eyck's *The Arnolfini Portrait*, a depiction of a merchant and what is thought to be his wife.

WHEN TO BULLSHIT
- When you're in Italy and would rather stay and eat more gelato instead of getting dragged to another museum.

BAROQUE
Getting more realistic and dramatic.
WHEN: 1600–1750

WHAT IT WAS
- Starting in Italy, baroque paintings, sculptures, and architecture reflected the religious tension between the Catholic Church and the Protestant Reformation.
- The Catholic Church used the art to engage people and act as propaganda in order to spread its religious doctrine.

- In Protestant areas, baroque art steered away from religion and focused on the growing middle class.

STYLES OF BAROQUE ART

- Baroque art in Catholic areas consisted of large paintings and frescos in order to gain the most viewers.
- The atmosphere was enhanced by selectively illuminating what was portrayed in the paintings and using deep shadows.
- Departing from the style of Renaissance art where the human form was idealized, baroque paintings portrayed realistic people.
- In Protestant areas, paintings portrayed activities of everyday life.
- Baroque architecture similarly made use of dramatic lighting.

BAROQUE ARTISTS AND ARTWORK

- Caravaggio—*David and Goliath*, depicting David as he stands over the giant he has just taken down. The scene illuminates the two realistic characters so that much of their bodies are hidden in the shadows.
- Rembrandt—*The Storm on the Sea of Galilee*, the only seascape by the artist, it depicts the apostles in the rough sea praying for help from Jesus.

INFORMATION TO USE WHEN BULLSHITTING

- Caravaggio used peasants to portray saints and apostles in his work.
- On March 18, 1990, *The Storm on the Sea of Galilee* and twelve other pieces were stolen from the Isabella Stewart Gardner Museum in Boston, Massachusetts. It is considered the largest art theft in U.S. history and remains unsolved to this day.

WHEN TO BULLSHIT

- When you want to sound well educated in the arts (drop Rembrandt into a conversation).
- When discussing how religion affects art.

IMPRESSIONISM

Briefly leaving their mark while dramatically changing art.
WHEN: 1867–1886

WHAT IT WAS

- Starting in France, impressionism was one of the first major shifts away from the traditions of painting.
- Artists placed emphasis on color and light instead of realism, often featuring loose brushstrokes and bright colors with less emphasis placed on form. The artists began depicting everyday modern life.
- Many impressionists would paint outside for a day, capturing a brief snapshot of the light. The result was an in-depth study of light and color.
- The name of the movement comes from an art critic who described Claude Monet's *Impression, Sunrise* as not being finished and just an impression of a painting.

ARTISTS AND ARTWORK

- Claude Monet—*Water Lilies*
- Édouard Manet—*A Bar at the Folies-Bergére*
- Pierre-Auguste Renoir—*Moulin de la Galette*

WHEN TO BULLSHIT

- When you want to impress with knowledge about modern art and French artists.
- When brought into a discussion about how painting has changed over time.

EXPRESSIONISM

It's about what's going on inside, not outside.
WHEN: 1905–1925

WHAT IT WAS

- Mostly known for the work produced out of Germany after the First World War, expressionism was the exact opposite of impressionism.

Where impressionists tried to show glimpses of the real world, expressionists attempted to portray the emotions, often extreme and distorted, of the artist or the subject.

- Expressionism placed great importance on the use of color and line to express emotion.
- Among the greatest influences of expressionism were the later works of Vincent van Gogh.

ARTISTS AND ARTWORK
- George Grosz—*The Funeral*
- Edvard Munch—*The Scream*
- Otto Dix—*Portrait of Dr. Heinrich Stadelmann*

INFORMATION TO USE WHEN BULLSHITTING
- Expressionism would move into other genres such as dance, architecture, and film. It would have a profound effect on Alfred Hitchcock, who featured expressionist themes in many of his films.

WHEN TO BULLSHIT
- When traveling In Europe or discussing artwork of Germany.
- When talking about life post-WWI.

CUBISM
Breaking down the image into its basic shapes.
WHEN: 1907–1914

WHAT IT WAS
- Cubism began in Paris as a response to break away from impressionism.
- It broke objects down into their more simple geometric shapes while also depicting different viewpoints.
- Cubism was heavily influenced by the works of Paul Cézanne, but led by Pablo Picasso and Georges Braque.

HERMETIC CUBISM

- Broke down the image even more, to the point that the subject of the painting was rendered unrecognizable.

SYNTHETIC CUBISM

- Incorporated the use of collage, where found objects like newspapers, advertisements, and flat pieces of paper were used instead of being painted.
- It combined high and low art.

CUBIST ARTWORK

- *Woman Playing the Mandolin* by Pablo Picasso—the subject of the painting is broken down into a series of basic shapes and shades.
- *Guernica* by Pablo Picasso—considered Picasso's greatest work, and one of the greatest works of the twentieth century, *Guernica* depicts the horrors of war in true cubist fashion.
- *Violin and Candlestick* by Georges Braque—depicts the three-dimensional objects in a flattened, fractured, and broken-down approach. By displaying many sides of the objects, he opened the viewers to different viewpoints.

WHEN TO BULLSHIT
- When talking about Picasso's contributions to the art world.
- When you want to impress someone by breaking down a painting.

DADAISM

The "anti-art" of art.
WHEN: 1916–1923

WHAT IT WAS

- Originating in Zurich, Switzerland, Dadaism was formed by a group of artists, writers, and intellectuals in response to World War I.
- Their reaction to the war was one of disgust and protest, and they classified their work as "anti-art."

- Dadaism was meant to destroy what the world knew as art and what the perceptions of art were.
- The work was meant to shock and elicit an emotional reaction.
- When World War I ended, several Dada artists brought the art form to other cities including Berlin, Paris, New York City, Tokyo, and Cologne.

RULE OF DADAISM
- Don't follow the rules of art.

DADA ARTISTS
- Marcel Duchamp
- Jean Arp
- George Grosz

FAMOUS WORKS OF ART
- Marcel Duchamp's *Fountain*—a urinal placed on its side and signed R. Mutt.
- Marcel Duchamp's *L.H.O.O.Q.*—a copy of the *Mona Lisa* with a mustache and goatee drawn on it. The title meant *Elle a chaud au cul*, which colloquially meant "She has a hot ass."

WHEN TO BULLSHIT
- The next time you're dragged to an art museum and have no clue what's going on (you can tell people to go to hell because you're a Dadaist).

SURREALISM
Art of the subconscious.
WHEN IT BEGAN: 1924

WHAT IT WAS
- Stemming from Dadaism, surrealism was founded by André Breton.
- Surrealism was heavily influenced by the works of Sigmund Freud and Carl Jung; the work focused on eliciting a response from the subconscious.

- Instead of displaying what was seen in the world like that of traditional artwork, surrealists created impossible landscapes and imagery in an attempt to open the mind and capture the human psyche.

ARTISTS AND ARTWORK
- *The Persistence of Memory* by Salvador Dalí
- *The Son of Man* by René Magritte
- *The Elephant Celebes* by Max Ernst

STORY TO USE WHEN BULLSHITTING
- Salvador Dalí, perhaps the most famous surrealist, worked in many other mediums besides paint.
- In one famous instance, Dalí attended a screening of the Surrealist film *Rose Hobart*. The film used clips from the movie *East of Borneo*, and specifically focused on its star, Rose Hobart, showing parts of Rose Hobart's scenes along with scenes from a documentary of an eclipse. Halfway through the screening, Dalí angrily stood up and knocked over the projector. Dalí claimed that he had the exact same idea for a movie and though he had never mentioned it or written it down, the film's director had stolen the idea from his subconscious and his dreams.

WHEN TO BULLSHIT
- When trying to sound thoughtful, deep, and intellectual.
- When trying to make sense of something that appears completely bizarre.

POP ART
Making popular culture artsy and appealing to the masses.
WHEN: 1955–1970

WHAT IT IS
- Starting in England and eventually moving to the United States, pop art was a response to abstract expressionism and the elitism it produced.

- Pop art used ideas and themes from popular culture like films, celebrities, advertisements, and television and focused on contemporary issues.
- Pop art was more understandable and related to a broader population, in particular, the youth of the 1950s and 1960s.
- Many artists used commercial printmaking techniques instead of painting.
- Pop art set out to show that art could be made out of nontraditional mediums, that the concept was more important than the physical piece of art, and rejected the notion of high art.

ANDY WARHOL
- The most well-known and influential pop artist.
- Much of his work dealt with familiar icons such as Campbell's Soup, Marilyn Monroe, and the atomic bomb.
- Warhol worked in many mediums, from paint, silkscreen, film, drawing, and photography.

INFORMATION TO USE WHEN BULLSHITTING
- The phrase 15 minutes of fame comes from Andy Warhol who said, "Anyone can be famous for 15 minutes."
- From 1966 to 1967, Warhol was the manager for The Velvet Underground and suggested they record an album with Nico, a German singer. Warhol helped secure the band a recording, and some of their most influential work was produced during this time period.

WHEN TO BULLSHIT
- Pop art is still very prevalent in fashion, accessories, and advertising. Use what you know to sound like you're in the know.

CONTEMPORARY ART
Art of today.
WHEN: 1960s–Now

WHAT IT IS
- Contemporary art is ongoing, and as such, has yet to truly be defined.

CONTEMPORARY ART MOVEMENT: NEO-POP

- In the 1980s, a renewed interest in pop art grew.
- In keeping with many of the themes of the original pop artists (such as celebrity and recognizable objects), neo-pop artists evaluate obsessions in Western culture and are often controversial.
- Example: Jeff Koons's *Michael Jackson and Bubbles*.

CONTEMPORARY ART MOVEMENT: STUCKISM

- A controversial art movement founded in 1999 to promote figurative painting and stray away from conceptual art.
- The group issued a series of manifestos in which they claimed to be replacing postmodernism with "remodernism."
- Example: Paul Harvey, *Punk Victorian*.

CONTEMPORARY ART MOVEMENT: PHOTOREALISM

- Photorealism began in the late 1960s.
- Artists use a camera to gain information, and they then replicate the picture with paint.
- Example: Chuck Close, *Self-Portrait*.

CONTEMPORARY ART MOVEMENT: TOYISM

- Begun in 1992, toyism paintings are colorful, tell a narrative, and appear humorous in nature, but deal with very real human emotions.
- Example: SRYLYN, *Live with Energy*.

WHEN TO BULLSHIT

- When talking to someone involved in the art world (you'll be able to keep up with the conversation and contribute).

Chapter 8

Film—Oscar Becomes Your BFF

SILENT ERA

Shh . . . the movies are starting.
WHEN: 1904–1928

THE EARLIEST DAYS OF FILM

- In 1890, William Dickson, Thomas Edison's assistant, created the first motion picture camera, called the kinetograph.
- The Lumiere brothers are credited as being the founding fathers of modern cinema. Creating their own portable camera, they filmed small, everyday scenes (called actuaries) and charged for viewings.
- Georges Méliès, a magician, created many films. His most notable film was *A Trip to the Moon* of 1902. Méliès was a pioneer in editing and special effects.
- In 1903, Edwin S. Porter's *The Great Train Robbery* came out. The film is one of the most influential films to have been produced in this era, showing the possibilities of narrative.

IMPORTANT SILENT FILMS

- 1915: *The Birth of a Nation* by D. W. Griffith—A three-hour saga most notably known for its achievements in narration and cinematography. The film faced great controversy because of its content, with the hero of the film being a member of the Ku Klux Klan.
- 1925: *The Battleship Potemkin* by Sergei Eisenstein—The story of a rebellious crew aboard a Russian battleship. It is most widely known for its use of fast-paced and precise editing.
- 1925: *The Gold Rush* by Charlie Chaplin—Chaplin's lovable tramp character goes to the Klondike in search of gold, and spends the harsh winter in a cabin.

TRANSITION INTO SOUND

- In 1927, *The Jazz Singer* became the first movie to incorporate sound.

WHEN TO BULLSHIT

- When making conversation with someone as the TV is muted and the silence is unbearable.

GOLDEN AGE

The studios take control.
AKA The Studio System
WHEN: 1928–1960s

WHO WAS INVOLVED

- Studios in "The Big Five" and "The Little Three"
- THE BIG FIVE
  - 20th Century Fox
  - Warner Bros
  - Paramount
  - RKO
  - Loew's (MGM)

- THE LITTLE THREE
  - Universal
  - Columbia
  - United Artists

WHAT IT WAS

- As sound was introduced into film, the major film studios started taking more control over all aspects of film, from production to distribution, even owning the movie theaters.
- Films were made on the studio's own lot, and writers, directors, and actors were often signed to long-term contracts.
- Studios had complete control over which theaters could get their films and would perform "block booking," in which they would sell multiple films at once in a block or unit to the theaters.
- Under block booking, theater owners purchased the films blindly.
- 1948: U.S. Supreme Court Case *United States v. Paramount Pictures, Inc.* outlawed block booking and the studios were ordered to give up their theaters.

FILMS OF THE GOLDEN AGE

- *It Happened One Night* and *Gone with the Wind*

STORY TO USE WHEN BULLSHITTING

- Both Clark Gable and Claudette Colbert were extremely unhappy about making *It Happened One Night* when they originally got the roles. According to the film's director, Frank Capra, the first time they met, Gable was drunk and rude to him.
- The film would later become the first comedy to sweep all five major categories of the Academy Awards.

WHEN TO BULLSHIT

- When talking with your grandparents about film and how movies "just haven't been the same" since their day.

MODERN CINEMA

Big movies, big sales (and small movies too).

WHAT IT IS

- Cinema of today is a blend of large, big budget films and small independent films.
- To produce the big budget films, the studios spend a lot of money in order to make a large profit in return.
- Foreign films, documentaries, and film festivals also play a key role in modern cinema.

LARGE-SCALE MOVIES

- *Jaws* is regarded as the first blockbuster film.
- Blockbusters have high production values and aim to appeal to the masses.
- An important aspect of the blockbuster is the franchising and selling of merchandize.
- Hollywood stars, name directors, sequels, special effects, remakes, and rereleases are another way to keep franchises going and to gain the most viewers.

SMALLER FILMS

- While large-scale films flourish, smaller, independent films also thrive.
- Film festivals like Tribeca and Sundance place emphasis on showcasing independent films and documentaries, and provide venues for distributors to purchase the films.

WHEN TO BULLSHIT

- When explaining why there's nothing but crap out nowadays.

INDEPENDENT FILM
Small budgets, big effects.

WHAT IT IS
- An independent film is any movie produced without the involvement of a major movie studio.
- Often these films have lower budgets.
- The 1990s saw a great rise and interest in independent films.
- Among many names to come out of this time are Richard Linklater (*Slackers*), Quentin Tarantino (*Reservoir Dogs*), Gus Van Sant (*Good Will Hunting*), and Kevin Smith (*Clerks*).

MIRAMAX
- Founded by Bob and Harvey Weinstein, Miramax was established as a distribution company for independent films.
- Steven Soderbergh's *Sex, Lies, and Videotape* put Miramax, and independent film as a whole, on the map.
- In 2000, Miramax was purchased by Disney.
- In 2005, the brothers left the company and created the Weinstein Company, which has gained great success and produced and distributed many films including *Inglourious Basterds* and *A Single Man*.

SOME INDIES TO TALK ABOUT
- *Kids*—Follows the lives of a group of kids living in New York City as they deal with sex, drugs, violence, rape, and HIV.
- *Reservoir Dogs*—Follows a group of robbers in a diamond heist that goes horribly wrong. The film only shows the events before and after the heist.

INFORMATION TO USE WHEN BULLSHITTING
- Harmony Korine, the writer of *Kids*, was only eighteen years old when he wrote the movie.
- *Good Will Hunting* was originally supposed to be a thriller, with Matt Damon's character becoming a secret agent for the government. Rob Reiner told Ben Affleck and Damon to lose the secret agent idea and to make the film about Will Hunting's relationship with his therapist.

WHEN TO BULLSHIT
- When trying to get your friends to go see that film that *isn't* 3D or with that actor you hate.

MOVIES TO KNOW
On being a film bluff.

CITIZEN KANE
- Considered to be one of the greatest films ever made.
- Directed by and starring Orson Welles, *Citizen Kane* tells the story of the rise and fall of Charles Foster Kane, a newspaper mogul.
- The film is narrated by flashbacks and opens with Kane on his deathbed, uttering the word "rosebud."
- At the end of the film, the viewer learns Rosebud was the sled Kane had as a child, the one time he was ever actually happy.

PSYCHO
- A thriller directed by Alfred Hitchcock.
- Marion Crane embezzles $40,000 from her boss and leaves to start a new life to be with her lover. She soon stops to rest at the Bates Motel, run by Norman Bates and his mother.
- The film is notable for having the protagonist killed halfway through the movie.
- The famous shower scene, in which the main character is murdered, has seventy-seven different camera angles.

RAGING BULL
- Biopic directed by Martin Scorsese depicting the turbulent life of boxer Jake LaMotta, starring Robert De Niro.
- Jake LaMotta's violence extends beyond the ring, and his life is often plagued with jealousy, rage, and paranoia, trusting no one including his wife and his brother.

THE GRADUATE

- The first film to truly express the voice of the baby boomer generation.
- Dustin Hoffman plays Benjamin Braddock, a recent college graduate who feels aimless and bored with life. As he begins having an affair with Mrs. Robinson (played by Anne Bancroft) he starts to fall in love with her daughter.

WHEN TO BULLSHIT

- When aiming to sound educated in film.
- When trying to impress your date before a movie begins.

NEW HOLLYWOOD

Making the baby boomers happy.
WHEN: 1967–1982

WHAT IT WAS

- Hollywood tries to gain appeal of the baby boomer generation.
- Films focused on younger themes including sex, music, and the counterculture.
- The rise of young, film school–educated filmmakers.
  - Steven Spielberg
  - Martin Scorsese
  - Woody Allen
  - Francis Ford Coppola
  - Robert Altman

BONNIE AND CLYDE

- One of the most well-known New Hollywood films.
- The film told the true story of two notorious bank robbers who were in love and were ultimately killed by the police in a bloody ambush.
- The film featured sex, romanticized violence, and social rebellion.
- The tag of the movie was "They're young, they're in love, they kill people."

THE END OF NEW HOLLYWOOD

- In 1975, *Jaws* came out, introducing audiences and film studios to the major blockbuster.
- Blockbusters allowed for mass appeal, and gave film studios different revenue streams such as merchandising and sequels.
- The New Hollywood era came to an end as film studios focused on making films with wider appeal and wide release.

WHEN TO BULLSHIT
- When attempting to sound edgy with your choice of film.

THE ACADEMY AWARDS
The granddaddy of all award shows.
AKA The Oscars

WHEN IT STARTED

- May 16, 1929: the first Academy Awards Ceremony is held at the Hotel Roosevelt in Hollywood, California.
- The ceremony, created by the American Academy of Motion Picture Arts and Sciences (AMPAS), was meant to recognize the achievements of members of the film industry, including actors, writers, and directors.

ABOUT OSCAR

- Official Name: The Academy Award of Merit.
- Created by sculptor George Stanley, the statuette depicts a knight holding a sword standing on a reel of film.
- The reel of film has five spokes, representing the five branches of the Academy: actors, writers, directors, producers, and technicians.
- The origins of the name Oscar are unclear.
- One belief is that Margaret Herrick, Academy executive secretary and future executive director, claimed the statue resembled her cousin, whom she called "Uncle Oscar."

- Another theory is the Bette Davis named it after her ex-husband, Harmon Oscar Nelson, Jr.
- In 1939, the Academy officially adopted "Oscar" as the name of the statuette.

WINNERS TO USE IN CONVERSATION
- 1991: *The Silence of the Lambs* won every major Academy Award
- 1969: *Midnight Cowboy* was the first and only X-rated film to win in the Best Picture category
- 2009: *The Hurt Locker* was the first and only film directed by a woman (Kathryn Bigelow) to win the Best Picture category

WHEN TO BULLSHIT
- When trying to impress your friends on your film knowledge.
- When you want to engage in conversation with the people around you, instead of suffering through another red carpet extravaganza with Joan Rivers.

ANIMATION
Making pictures move.

WHAT IT IS
- Sequence of images to create the illusion of motion.

TRADITIONAL ANIMATION
- Hand drawn on paper and then transferred to transparent sheets called cels.
- Example: *Beauty and the Beast*.

STOP-MOTION
- The process of manipulating an object and photographing one frame at a time to create motion.
- Example: *The Nightmare Before Christmas*.

3D ANIMATION
- Motion is simulated by manipulating a 3D digital model.
- Example: *Toy Story.*

WALT DISNEY, 1901–1966
- A pioneer in animation, taking cartoons away from a "rubber hose" style and making characters look and feel more realistic.
- *Flowers and Trees* was the first cartoon with color.
- *Steamboat Willie* (featuring Mickey Mouse) was the first cartoon to have synchronized sound.
- *Snow White and the Seven Dwarfs* was the first full-length animated film.

TEX AVERY, 1908–1980
- Creator of Bugs Bunny, Daffy Duck, and Porky Pig.
- Steered animation away from Disney's style and made cartoons more enjoyable for adults.
- His work included sarcasm, humor, exaggerated slapstick, and the cartoons were self-referential, often breaking the fourth wall.

PIXAR
- Brought computer-generated imagery (CGI) to the forefront of animation while still emphasizing the importance of story and character.
- *Toy Story* was released in 1995, and was the first full-length feature film entirely in CGI.
- To date, the studio has earned twenty-four Academy Awards.

WHEN TO BULLSHIT
- When standing in line with your girlfriend and her little brother for that movie he's been dying to see.

THE MPAA
This film is rated . . . BS.
AKA The Motion Picture Association of America

WHAT IT DOES
- The MPAA is a nonprofit organization that administers the film rating system of G, PG, PG-13, R, and NC-17 (at one time referred to as X).
- The ratings are only the personal opinions of members and are meant to be a suggestion for parents with regard to what movies their children should see.
- Theater owners agree to enforce the ratings.

WHO THEY ARE
- The ratings and appeals board members are kept under a shroud of secrecy.
- The MPAA claims to hire only parents with children ages five to seventeen and that raters do not receive any form of training.

CONTROVERSY
- When a movie is given an NC-17, many theaters will refuse to show the film.
- As a result, movies tone down their content or remove scenes entirely to avoid the NC-17 rating.
- Many have raised concerns over what material receives an R and what material receives NC-17.
- For example, films showing oral sex on a male will receive an R rating; however, if performed on a woman, the film will receive an NC-17.

INTERESTING FACT TO USE WHEN BULLSHITTING
- Upon complaints that *Indiana Jones and the Temple of Doom* had too much gore for a film rated PG, Steven Spielberg suggested they create PG-13, a rating between PG and R.
- The movie *This Film Is Not Yet Rated* explores the MPAA in great detail, showcasing its fallacies and even going so far as to expose who the members are.

WHEN TO BULLSHIT
- When explaining to someone why that scene with the blood-filled orgy might be the reason for the NC-17.

NEW TECHNOLOGIES

Hi-tech films, low-tech explanation.

FILM HAS ALWAYS HAD TO ADAPT

- Film is a medium that is constantly adapting to the new technologies of the time.
- From the transition to sound and color, to the transition from film to digital, the medium constantly has to change to keep up with the technology of the present day.
- The film industry not only has to change with technology, but take advantage of what new technologies have to offer.

3D TECHNOLOGY

- Many 3D movies were wildly popular in the 1950s, but were considered to be a fad that died out quickly. They briefly resurfaced in the 1980s; however, they didn't last long.
- James Cameron's 2009 film, *Avatar*, presented a new outlook on the future of films in 3D.
- Cameron used a new 3D-camera system that not only filmed in 3D, but allowed the director to view the footage with the CGI in real time.

IMAX

- IMAX is a film format with the capabilities of filming and displaying films of greater size and resolution.
- The largest movie screen in the world is in the LG IMAX Theater in Sydney, South Wales. It stands eight stories high, covering an area of more than 10,930 square feet.
- IMAX announced in early January 2010 that a 3D IMAX camera was in the works.

WHEN TO BULLSHIT
- When trying to sound technologically savvy.
- When you need to impress someone with your knowledge of how the film industry is evolving.

Chapter 9

Television—Boob Tube Schooling

HOW IT WORKS

Getting the picture.

CATHODE RAY TUBE
- Cathode ray tube is used in standard-definition television.
- A cathode, a filament that when heated creates electrons, is placed in a vacuum (tube).
- The ray is a stream of electrons that comes off the cathode and into the vacuum.
- A high beam is created, and hits the flat screen at the end of the vacuum.
- The screen is coated in phosphor, and when the beam hits, it glows.
- An image is created by lighting different areas of the coated screen.

PLASMA
- Plasma televisions do not have a cathode ray tube.
- The image is created by lighting up tiny dots, or pixels, with a gas called plasma that reacts with an electrical charge.

LIQUID CRYSTAL DISPLAY (LCD)
- When an electrical current is produced, light crystals between two sheets of polarized-glass plate open and block the passage of light.

HIGH DEFINITION

- HDTV has an aspect ratio of 16:9, compared to standard television's 4:3 aspect ratio.
- While standard definition completes the image every twenty-four frames per second, HD completes the image every sixty frames per second.

WHEN TO BULLSHIT

- When shopping for a new television—sounding like you know *exactly* what's going on will help make sure you don't get swindled.

CLASSIC VERSUS MODERN
Something old, something new.

THE FIRST GOLDEN AGE OF TELEVISION (1949–1960)
- Early sitcoms represented the American nuclear family as perfect.
  - Example: *Leave it to Beaver, Father Knows Best*
- Live hour-long dramas were based on plays, anthology dramas became incredibly popular, and many big names of the time were associated with programming.
  - Example: *Alfred Hitchcock Presents, NBC Television Playhouse*
- Only the major three networks existed, and programming was transmitted twelve to eighteen hours a day.

THE SECOND GOLDEN AGE OF TELEVISION (1980S–PRESENT?)
- Many believe we are currently in a new Golden Age of Television.
- Sitcoms of today have reshaped the idea of what family is.
- *Friends, Seinfeld*, and *The Office* depict families outside of the nuclear model.
- There are no longer just three networks vying for viewers' attention. With the rise of cable, programs have become more provocative, thought provoking, and cutting edge.
  - Example: *The Sopranos, The Wire, Lost, It's Always Sunny in Philadelphia*

- Dramatic programming has become serialized, even with the same production values of film, and programming strategies have become a crucial part in targeting demographics.
- Reality television has become a staple to television programming.

WHEN TO BULLSHIT
- When explaining to someone why you enjoy watching a particular program.

GAME SHOWS
A genre in jeopardy.

THE HISTORY
- Before television came along, game shows were a prominent part of radio in the 1930s.
- *Spelling Bee* was the first game show to be broadcast on television.
- Game shows appealed to producers because of the relatively low production cost, and the live filming created great drama for the viewers at home.

THE QUIZ SHOW SCANDAL
- In 1956, Herb Stempel won $69,500 on the television show *Twenty-One*. He was then approached by the show's producer and told to throw the game to the new, younger contestant, Charles Van Doren, which he did.
- Stempel came out with the story, and eventually other contestants came out with the truth that they had been given the answers to questions, and that the shows had been fixed.
- In 1959, Congress held hearings over the scandal, and on November 2, Van Doren, who had denied cheating, came forward and admitted his guilt.

RESULT OF THE QUIZ SHOW SCANDAL

- Producers blamed the scandal on pressure from advertisers, and as a result, got rid of the single-sponsorship model, replacing it with the commercial model that is still in place today.
- Congress declared rigging game shows a federal crime.

WHEN TO BULLSHIT

- To show someone you have an in-depth knowledge of the very popular genre.
- When trying to impress your girlfriend as you watch *Jeopardy!* together.
- When arguing why *Wheel of Fortune* and *Deal or No Deal* should not be on television because they require absolutely no skill.

ADVERTISING

What you see is what they want you to get.

THE PURPOSE OF ADVERTISING

- Advertising pays for the costs of the programs on television.
- Certain time slots are sold to advertisers by the networks to appeal to their target demographic.
- The higher the ratings for a program, the more a network can charge for an advertisement.

ADVERTISING IN TODAY'S WORLD

- With the invention of digital video recorders (DVRs) and more people viewing their content online, advertisers and television networks have had to find a way to keep ads relevant and make sure people are tuning in to them.

ADVERTISING STRATEGIES

- Advertisers use several strategies to ensure that people will watch.
- Harkening back to a method used in the early days of radio, many television shows will now include product placement directly within the television program.

- There is no clearer example of this than *American Idol*. The show is practically one long, big commercial for Coca-Cola. Even if one fast-forwards through the commercials, it will be absolutely impossible to miss Coke's stamp.
- Advertisers also use other methods such as celebrity endorsements, sponsorship, pop-up ads, and interactive advertisements online.

WHEN TO BULLSHIT
- When trying to explain the workings of advertising.
- When trying to impress your boss with advertising ideas for your company.

SITCOMS
The situation with comedies.

HOW THEY BEGAN
- Situational comedies have roots dating back to the days of radio.
- When television first came on the scene, many radio stars and their shows simply made the transition onto television.
- Filmed in front of a studio audience, the original sitcoms were filmed and aired live.

LUCY CHANGES THINGS
- *I Love Lucy* brought many significant changes to the sitcom.
- Instead of being taped live, the show was recorded on film.
- The show was also the first show to use the three-camera setup, where three cameras were placed along the set and filmed the action from different viewpoints. The material would later be edited together.
- The three-camera setup has become a staple to sitcoms and is still used today.

CHANGING THROUGH THE TIMES
- Sitcoms of the 1960s were fantastical.
- Shows such as *I Dream of Genie*, *Bewitched*, and *The Munsters* strayed away from real life.

- As the baby-boomer generation grew in the 1970s, sitcoms started reflecting the things that mattered most to them.
- Shows focused on controversial issues such as race, sexuality, and war.
  - Examples: *M*A*S*H*, *All in the Family*, and *Soap*.

SITCOMS TODAY

- Sitcoms today are a combination of the three-camera system (filmed in front of a live studio audience and featuring a laugh track) and the single-camera system (one camera and no laugh track).

WHEN TO BULLSHIT
- When you want to fill the commercial time with conversation.
- When trying to understand the appeal of *Two and a Half Men* (seriously).

DRAMAS

When programs get serious.

DURING THE GOLDEN AGE OF TELEVISION

- Hour-long dramas flourished from 1949 to 1960, and consisted of teleplays, and live works adapted from the stage.
  - Example: *Kraft Television Theatre*

WESTERNS

- Westerns were a popular form of radio programming and made the transition into television.
- *Gunsmoke* began in 1952 on the radio and is the longest lasting television show of all time. The series ended its twenty-year run in 1975.
- Though traditional westerns like *Bonanza* and *Gunsmoke* have disappeared, there has been a resurgence with shows like HBO's *Deadwood* and Fox's *Firefly*, which combined the genre with science fiction.

SOAP OPERAS

- The term "soap opera" came from the early days in radio when programs had soap companies such as Procter & Gamble as their sponsors.

- Soap operas are notable for their series. Episodes are not self-contained story arches, but rather part of a larger, continuing narrative.
- Canceled in 2009, *Guiding Light* was the oldest running soap opera, with a seventy-two-year run.

CRIME SHOWS

- *Dragnet* was a pioneer in the crime show genre, presenting police and legal issues with an authenticity never before seen.
- Steven Bochco is one of the most well-known creators of crime shows, responsible for *NYPD Blue*, *Hill Street Blues*, *L.A. Law*, and the failed *Cop Rock*, which was one part cop show, one part musical.

MINISERIES

- In a miniseries, a single story is told over the course of episodes.
- Miniseries have shorter seasons than normal programming.
- One of the most renowned miniseries was *Roots*, which aired in 1977.

WHEN TO BULLSHIT

- When everyone's talking about last night's episode of *that* show, you can add your two cents worth.

REALITY TV

Too real for comfort.

HOW IT BEGAN

- In 1947, *Candid Microphone* (which would later become *Candid Camera*) aired. The show put everyday people in funny situations.
- In 1963, the Public Broadcasting System (PBS) aired *American Family*, a three-part documentary that followed a family as they dealt with issues of homosexuality and divorce. *American Family* dropped the formal sit-down interviews and used portable cameras.
- In the 1970s and much of the 1980s, reality programming was lighthearted and focused on humorous stories of people.

WHEN THINGS STARTED TO CHANGE

- In 1988, Fox aired *COPS* in response to the Writers Guild strike. The series followed police officers on their everyday routines and featured no interviews or music, along with the use of hand-held cameras. The show became wildly successful.
- In 1992, MTV aired *The Real World*, which followed seven people living together while dealing with issues of drugs, sexuality, and racism.
- From *The Real World* came *Road Rules*, which applied the contest aspect to reality programs.

REALITY TODAY

- In 2000, *Survivor* took contestants out of their comfort zones to compete against one another. The resulting plotting, scheming, and forming of alliances had never been seen before.
- In 2002, *American Idol* paved the way for a new kind of reality show that encouraged at-home audience participation.
- The documentary-style programming continued to showcase a variety of subjects, from makeovers to celebrity life.

WHEN TO BULLSHIT

- When arguing that *Keeping Up with the Kardashians* is a part of an important, groundbreaking genre in television that deserves the utmost respect (good luck with that).

NETWORKS

There were NBC, ABC, and CBS . . . until someone else came along.

THE BEGINNING OF TELEVISION

- Television ran on a commercial-based model akin to radio.
- Early programming was taken from shows already existing in radio.
- As time progressed, programming and technology came into their own and the major three networks had the majority of shows being offered on television.

- These networks catered to a mass audience, with the goal of gaining the most viewers.

THE MAJOR THREE NETWORKS
- The major three networks originated in the early days of radio. ABC, once known as NBC Blue, broke apart from NBC due to a Supreme Court hearing.
- NBC (National Broadcasting Company).
- ABC (American Broadcasting Company).
- CBS (Columbia Broadcasting System).

A FOURTH NETWORK BREAKS THROUGH
- In 1987, the Fox Network launched.
- To gain viewers, Fox focused on the niche market, or the underrepresented viewers like African Americans and the youth.
- Their shows reflected edgy and young programming such as *The Tracey Ullman Show*, *The Simpsons*, and *Married . . . with Children*.
- In 1993, Fox gained a contract with the National Football League.
- After one season, the number of viewers peaked dramatically, establishing Fox as a new, fourth network.

WHEN TO BULLSHIT
- While channel surfing.

CABLE
TV just got a whole lot bigger.

HOW IT BEGAN
- Cable, originally called Community Antenna Television (CATV), was invented to enhance television reception in areas with weak signals.
- Often, those affected with weak signals were people living in mountainous areas or remote locations.
- A series of antennae were connected from house to house, leading to an antenna tower on the top of a mountain.

- In the 1950s, cable operators could pick up signals from hundreds of miles away in other states, which provided a new variety of programming.

FCC FREEZE
- In 1948, the Federal Communications Commission put a freeze on granting television licenses.
- The freeze would last for four years.
- The freeze created an opportunity for cable to gain viewers and by 1952, CATV had 14,000 subscribers.

PAY TV
- In 1972, Service Electronic offered Home Box Office (HBO) their system in Pennsylvania.
- With the success and rise of pay TV stations, and the invention of the satellite dish, more and more people paid to view their programming.

A CABLE WORLD
- Today's world is no longer dominated by the big three networks.
- There are literally hundreds of channels to watch, and hundreds of demographics for advertisers to chase.

WHEN TO BULLSHIT
- When discussing how cable is much better than satellite.
- When discussing the quality of cable programming compared to network television.

SCHEDULING PROGRAMS
The art of making you watch and keep watching.

WHAT IT IS
- Scheduling uses methods to attract the most viewers to a specific program and retain them.
- It is used to present the programming when the audience would want to watch in order to retain viewership.

- It seeks to make sure advertising is the most effective for that demographic.

BLOCK PROGRAMMING
- Running several programs consecutively, all generated for the same audience.
  - Example: Must-See TV Thursday on NBC.
- Thursday nights dedicated solely to comedy programs.

COUNTERPROGRAMMING
- Running a show that targets a different audience from the competing networks.
  - Example: On Sunday nights, ABC runs *Desperate Housewives* to appeal to the women demographic as NBC runs *Sunday Night Football* to appeal to the male demographic.

BRIDGING
- Having a program end later so that the other networks' programming has already started.
- This persuades viewers to stay on the channel they were watching because they have already missed part of the show on the other networks.

SWEEPS
- Several times during the year, Nielsen Media Research will conduct research to record viewing figures.
- By informing the networks which shows get the most viewers, they are then able to charge more for advertising.
- Networks pack the programming with special episodes and events to gain the most viewers.
  - Example: Season finales, guest stars, or special episodes.

WHEN TO BULLSHIT
- When you need a response for your coworker who questions why he stayed up late to watch that crappy show the night before.

Chapter 10

Books— *Of Course* I've Read That

MYSTERY
Who dun the "Whodunnits."

EDGAR ALLAN POE
- Considered to be the father of mystery, in 1841, Edgar Allan Poe published the first mystery book, *The Murders in the Rue Morgue*.
- 'The book follows C. Auguste Dupin as he tries to solve a case the police deemed unsolvable.

SIR ARTHUR CONAN DOYLE AND SHERLOCK HOLMES
- Perhaps the most well-known detective in the history of literature.
- Holmes and Watson were introduced to audiences in 1887 in *A Study in Scarlet*.
- Sherlock Holmes made his deductions based on extreme intelligence and scientific principles.

OTHER AUTHORS TO USE IN CONVERSATION
- Agatha Christie—one of the most well-known mystery writers, Christie wrote over eighty novels.
- Edward Stratemeyer—author of both the *Nancy Drew* and *The Hardy Boys* series.
- Dashiell Hammett—author of *The Thin Man* series and *The Maltese Falcon*.

BOOKS TO TALK ABOUT
- *The Mystery of Edwin Drood* by Charles Dickens—a mystery with truly no answer due to the author's untimely death before finishing the book.
- *The Killer Inside Me* by Jim Thompson—a dark tale of a sheriff of a small town who plays dumb and hides his sociopath tendencies.

WHEN TO BULLSHIT
- When hitting on someone in a library.
- When being dragged to a book club.
- When confronted with the question "Why don't you stop watching television and read something?"

HORROR

The words are scary, but the bullshit isn't.

WHAT IT IS
- A literary genre intended to elicit feelings of fear, dread, or dismay in its readers.
- Horror literature takes on many forms and deals with topics ranging from the mundane to the supernatural.

IMPORTANT AUTHOR: H. P. LOVECRAFT (1890–1937)
- Though relatively unknown during his lifetime, Lovecraft has become a cult figure in horror literature and is considered to be the twentieth century Edgar Allan Poe.
- He is most recognized for his "Cthulhu Mythos," the shared literary world in which he and various authors set works of horror.

- Important stories include: "The Unnamable," "The Call of Cthulhu," "The Colour out of Space."

IMPORTANT AUTHOR: STEPHEN KING (1947–PRESENT)

- The most important horror author in the past forty years, Stephen King has won six Bram Stoker awards, six Horror Guild awards, five Locus awards, three World Fantasy awards, and a Lifetime Achievement Award.
- His books have sold more than 300 million copies, and most have been adapted for television and film.
- Important works include: *Carrie*, *Salem's Lot*, *The Shining*, *Cujo*, *The Stand*, *It*.

IMPORTANT AUTHOR: RICHARD MATHESON (1926–PRESENT)

- Richard Matheson is considered to be one of the greatest horror writers not influenced by the work of H. P. Lovecraft.
- He is best known for "What Dreams May Come," "Bid Time Return," "Duel," and "I Am Legend," all of which have become major motion pictures.
- Other Matheson stories turned into films or TV episodes include: "The Incredible Shrinking Man," "Stir of Echoes," and "Hell House" (*The Legend of Hell House*).
- Stephen King cites Matheson as the author who influenced him the most.

THE CLASSICS

- *Frankenstein* by Mary Shelley
- *The Strange Case of Dr. Jekyll and Mr. Hyde* by Robert Louis Stevenson
- *Dracula* by Bram Stoker

WHEN TO BULLSHIT

- When talking with or wooing a Goth.
- When talking about a book (you haven't read) before seeing its inevitable movie version.

SCIENCE FICTION AND FANTASY
Authors writing out of this world.

RAY BRADBURY
- Bradbury has more than 500 published pieces of work, including books, television scripts, and plays.
- His most famous novel is *Fahrenheit 451*, a dystopian novel about a firefighter with the job of setting books, and the homes of people with books, on fire. Slowly, his views on the hedonistic world around him begin to fall apart.

JULES VERNE
- Verne is considered a pioneer of science fiction.
- Verne is most known for his works *Twenty Thousand Leagues under the Sea*, *Journey to the Center of the Earth*, and *From the Earth to the Moon*.
- Verne, a French author, had received poor reviews of his work in the United States because of his poor writing. It was not until the 1960s that proper translations appeared.

H. G. WELLS
- Along with Verne, Wells is considered to be the "Father of Science Fiction." His notable works include *The Invisible Man*, *The Island of Doctor Moreau*, *The Time Machine*, and *The War of the Worlds*.
- In 1938, Orson Welles and the Mercury Theatre on the Air adapted *The War of the Worlds* as a radio program. The program brought on mass panic from the people listening, many who feared an actual alien invasion was taking place.

WHEN TO BULLSHIT
- When making conversation with a Trekkie or Dungeons and Dragons player.

NONFICTION
You might not be telling the truth, but the books are.

IN COLD BLOOD
- *In Cold Blood* came out in 1966 and is considered by critics to be the first nonfiction novel.
- More known for his romantic works like *Breakfast at Tiffany's*, Truman Capote wanted to work in nonfiction. He chose as his subject the 1959 murders of Herbert Clutter and his wife and two children in the town of Holcomb, Kansas.
- Capote's research lasted five years, and the book tells the stories of both the victims and the murderers.

BLACK BOY
- The autobiography of Richard Wright, an African American, who while growing up in the South of the 1920s, not only experiences extreme racism and violence, but also oppression of his intellect. He eventually moves to Chicago where he finds racial tensions to be much less extreme, and becomes a member of the Communist Party. He comes to the realization that the Communist Party is also full of fearful people who are not willing to accept change and new ideas, and disillusioned he leaves the party.

THE EDUCATION OF HENRY ADAMS
- Henry Adams is the great-grandson of John Adams, and the grandson of John Quincy Adams.
- In his autobiography (which he tells in the third person), he explores the meaning of life and how his formal Harvard education did not prepare him for the real world.

WHEN TO BULLSHIT
- When trying to impress someone with your taste in books.

HISTORICAL FICTION
Rewriting history.

WHAT IT IS
- Historical fiction tells a fictional story that takes place in an actual period from the past.

MEMOIRS OF A GEISHA
- Written by Arthur Golden, an American man from Tennessee, the book is a rags-to-riches story, telling the first-person account of a Japanese woman working as a geisha before and after the Second World War.

THE PENELOPIAD
- Written by Margaret Atwood, *The Penelopiad* retells Homer's *The Odyssey* from the point of view of his wife, Penelope, and her twelve maids that Odysseus would later hang. The book tries to answer the question of what Penelope really was up to all those years Odysseus was away, and why when he returned, he decided to kill her maids.

THE CLAN OF THE CAVE BEAR
- The first of six books by Jean M. Auel, the story follows early humans and the interactions between Neanderthals and Cro-Magnons during the Ice Age. The story focuses particularly on Ayla, a young Cro-Magnon girl who is taken in by a Neanderthal tribe.

A TALE OF TWO CITIES
- Written by Charles Dickens, *A Tale of Two Cities* is one of the most famous historical-fiction novels. The book takes place in Paris and London, before and after the French Revolution, and follows a series of people throughout the years as the social unrest grows.

WHEN TO BULLSHIT
- When you want to make conversation with history buffs and bookworms alike.

COMIC BOOKS & GRAPHIC NOVELS

A lot more than just the Sunday funnies.

HISTORY OF COMIC BOOKS

- *Hogan's Alley*, the first comic strip, was published on May 5, 1895.
- The first comic book was published in 1933, and was mainly a collection of reprints of comics found in newspapers.
- In June of 1938, ACTION COMICS #1 was published, with the very first appearance of Superman.
- During this time, the world was introduced to characters such as Captain America, Batman, and Wonder Woman.

ALAN MOORE

- A major name in the world of graphic novels, Moore is the writer of one of the most critically acclaimed series, *Watchmen*, a dark deconstruction of the comic book superhero.

BUT NOT ALL COMIC BOOKS ARE ABOUT SUPERHEROS

- In 1976, Harvey Pekar, with artist Robert Crumb, created *American Splendor*, a comic book that told autobiographical stories and everyday tales of Pekar living in Cleveland.

INFORMATION TO USE WHEN BULLSHITTING

- In 1954, Dr. Frederick Wertham published an article "proving" that comic books turned juvenile delinquents into criminals. As a result, the Supreme Court held hearings and comic publishers came together and created the Comics Code, which provided certain bans in comic books (such as werewolves, zombies, and vampires).

WHEN TO BULLSHIT

- When attending Comic-Con.

BESTSELLERS

The ones everybody reads (except you).

THE DA VINCI CODE

- Dan Brown's book centers around symbology Professor Robert Langdon, who attempts to solve the murder of a curator of the Louvre. The curator's curious death, as well as the marks left on and around his body, set in motion a trail of clues that lay hidden in the works of Leonardo Da Vinci. As the mystery unravels, the clues lead Langdon and Sophie (the curator's niece), to what they believe to be the Holy Grail.
- In the end, we discover that Sophie's family is of the bloodline of Jesus and Mary Magdalene, and that she is the only descendant still alive.

TO KILL A MOCKINGBIRD

- Harper Lee's book is centered in a small Alabama town during the Great Depression. Scout, a six-year-old girl, lives with her brother and their widowed father, Atticus, a lawyer. Scout, her brother, and their friend become intrigued by their reclusive neighbor, Boo Radley, and try to gain his attention from within his home.
- Atticus takes on a case defending Tom, a black man who is accused of raping a white woman. Despite the evidence, Tom is found guilty and on his way out of the courthouse, is shot dead. Bob Ewell, the town drunk who was caught lying in the trial, vows revenge on Atticus.
- That Halloween, Scout and her brother are attacked by a man, but a mysterious man comes to their rescue and brings them home. They realize it is Boo Radley. When they get home, the police tell Atticus that Bob Ewell has been killed.

THE GIRL WITH THE DRAGON TATTOO

- Steig Larsson's main character, Mikael Blomkvist, is a journalist in the middle of a libel case, who is called on by a rich industrialist. He is told to find out what happened to Harriet, a woman who had gone missing from his estate forty years ago and who he believes was murdered.
- Blomkvist is aided by Lisbeth Salander, a twenty-four-year-old computer hacker. The two discover that Harriet's brother had been raping and murdering women for years, and that it had been initiated by their

father, who sexually abused them as kids. Mikael and Lisbeth discover that Harriet was not in fact murdered, but had fled the country.

WHEN TO BULLSHIT
- When you need to sound like you stay current with the books of today.
- When making someone believe you love to read.

POETRY

There's more than just words.

MAYA ANGELOU, "PHENOMENAL WOMEN"
- This poem deals with the issues of perceived beauty.
- The poem presents a woman revealing her secrets of what makes her phenomenal. It is not about the way she looks, but her personality.

ROBERT FROST, "THE ROAD NOT TAKEN"
- The speaker stands in the woods in front of a fork in the road.
- After analyzing the two paths, he discerns no difference between the two.
- The speaker chooses one of the paths, claiming that he would return to the other path at a later date, though he knows this probably isn't true.
- The speaker says one day he will tell this story with a sigh, claiming he chose the path less traveled.
- The ending of the poem has sparked great debate. Some believe it to be a sigh of relief, while others believe it to be a sigh of regret.
- The poem represents the unknown of the future, and how the decisions we make in life shape our paths.

E. E. CUMMINGS, "I CARRY YOUR HEART"
- He was a master when it came to playing with words in a visual and experimental way.
- "i carry your heart," a poem about a deep and profound love, is a perfect example of cummings's use of enjambment (continuing a sentence beyond the end of the line) and his use of punctuation (where he uses parentheses throughout the poem).

COOKBOOKS
Mastering the art of BS in the kitchen.

THE JOY OF COOKING
- There have been eight editions since the Great Depression.
- The first edition, self-published in 1931, featured sections on how to pickle, and how to use meats like squirrel and opossum.
- The 2006 edition features 4,500 recipes.
- All of the books have been written by Irma Rombauer or members of her family.

MASTERING THE ART OF FRENCH COOKING
- This bestseller paved the way for Julia Child's successful career as a pioneer TV chef.
- The ingredients required in the book are easy to find; however, Child's great attention to technique is what sets this book apart from others.
- One of Child's most famous dishes is her beef bourguignon.

MOOSEWOOD COOKBOOK
- Originally published in 1977, Mollie Katzen's *Moosewood Cookbook* is, according to the *New York Times*, one of the bestselling cookbooks of all time.
- The book is based on the vegetarian recipes from Katzen's restaurant, Moosewood Restaurant.
- The book is said to have revolutionized vegetarian cuisine.

TRAVEL
Getting around.

WHAT IS TRAVEL LITERATURE?
- Travel literature can be broken down into two categories.
  - Travel guides—guidebooks with information and helpful tips about a specific place one might visit.
  - Travel narratives—nonfiction narratives detailing an author's experience while traveling.

EXAMPLES OF TRAVEL GUIDES
- *Lonely Planet*—caters to students and those who wish to travel on a budget. *Lonely Planet* also caters to those who are more adventurous.
- *Frommer's*—intended for older people, with detailed history and hotel recommendations.
- *Fodor's*—also intended for older people, with a detailed history and recommendations, but also providing unusual spots to visit.

EXAMPLES OF TRAVEL NARRATIVES
- *The Lost Continent: Travels in Small Town America* by Bill Bryson—a comedic account of one man who travels across the United States in search of the perfect small town.
- *Four Corners: A Journey into the Heart of Papua New Guinea* by Kira Salak—Salak travels across the remote island encountering cannibals and meeting the leader of a guerilla movement.
- *Arabia, a Journey Through the Labyrinth* by Jonathan Raban—tells the story of Raban's travels through the Arab world, telling stories of both the rich and the poor.

WHEN TO BULLSHIT
- When you need to sound worldly.

Chapter 11

Economics— Bean Counters Be Damned

MICROECONOMICS

Economics of the individual.

WHAT IT IS

- Focuses on the role individual consumers, households, and firms play in the economy.
- Looks at when consumers purchase goods, and the price at which goods are sold.

UTILITY

- Benefit or satisfaction from an item or good.
- The more benefit, the more consumers are willing to pay.
- Marginal utility: The amount of satisfaction one unit of a good will bring.
- As more of a good is consumed, the marginal utility decreases.
- Total utility: The summation of the marginal utilities.
  - For example: With the first piece of cake, the marginal utility will be high. But when the sixth piece comes along, the total utility will be low.

OPPORTUNITY COST

- Method of measuring cost through identifying another alternative use of that money.
- The lost profit from the alternative situation is the opportunity cost.
  - For example: If a person decides to eat out at an expensive restaurant instead of staying home and cooking, the opportunity cost is what that money could have been used for in the future.
- When consumers or businesses buy or create goods, they are risking the chance of not buying or creating another good. This is their opportunity cost.

MARKET FAILURE

- Any situation that will disturb the competitive market.
- This affects pricing of goods.
  - For example: If a company has a monopoly on a good, they can raise the prices without consequence because there are no other goods like that on the market.

WHEN TO BULLSHIT

- When deciding whether to go to Costco and buy in bulk or hold out one more day at your local supermarket.
- When advising someone about how he should spend his money.

MACROECONOMICS

Making the economy grow.

WHAT IT IS

- Study of national economy or regional economies, focusing on what causes the economy to grow or fluctuate, changes in employment or unemployment, performance of international trade, and the result of economic policies.
- Macroeconomists try to predict economic conditions to better prepare governments, firms, and consumers for the future.
- Uses microeconomics to understand the bigger picture.

GROSS DOMESTIC PRODUCT (GDP)

- Total value of goods and services produced in a year within the country.
- Most commonly used indicator on economic behavior.

GROSS NATIONAL PRODUCT (GNP)

- Total value of goods and services produced by residents from a country, even if they are living abroad. Outsourcing and foreign firms within a country are included in the GNP, however not in the GDP.

INFLATION AND UNEMPLOYMENT

- Inflation is the continual rise in prices of a good. As a result, the value of the dollar does not remain the same.
- Unemployment reduces GDP.

FISCAL POLICY

- Government decisions pertaining to taxation and spending with the goal of having economic growth.

MONETARY POLICY

- Regulation of interest rates and supply of money to ensure sustainable growth.
- Set by the U.S. Federal Reserve.

WHEN TO BULLSHIT

- When you want to sound like you understand how the bigger picture of economics works.

SUPPLY AND DEMAND

You want it, and they want to give it to you.

WHAT IT IS

- Supply and demand is one of the most fundamental concepts in understanding economics.

- Supply pertains to how much of a good is available.
- Demand pertains to how much of a good people want.
- The price of a good or service is a direct reflection of supply and demand combined.

THE LAW OF SUPPLY

- As the price of a good increases, the quantity of that good increases and vice versa.
- Supply is sensitive to time, meaning long and short term. If the demand or price changes, the supply has to be able to react accordingly.

THE LAW OF DEMAND

- As the price of a good increases, the demand from the consumer will decrease and vice versa.

EQUILIBRIUM AND DISEQUILIBRIUM

- When both supply and demand are equal, the economy is at equilibrium. This means the amount of goods supplied is equal to the amount being demanded.
- Equilibrium is only an economic theory, and cannot be achieved in the real market place.
- Disequilibrium is when the amount supplied does not equal the amount demanded at the definite price.

WHEN TO BULLSHIT
- When starting your own business, it's crucial to have an understanding of supply and demand (or at least appear to).

SPECIALIZATION
Sticking to what you do well.

WHAT IT IS
- When people or organizations focus production efforts on a limited number of tasks.

- Workers only perform tasks they are most skilled at, leaving other job opportunities available.
- On a macroeconomic level, countries focus on producing the most advantageous goods and trade with other countries for any other goods.

DIVISION OF LABOR

- Specialization is directly related to the concept of division of labor, where, like an assembly line, a complicated amount of work is broken down into smaller, easier parts for individuals.
- Specialization can come into play when choosing the correct job for the individual.
- Division of labor shortens the production time and increases the amount of products made.

WHY SPECIALIZATION WORKS

- Having a worker or company focus on one thing they are good at speeds up production time because they don't have to focus on another, separate task.
- Specialization will eventually increase quantities.
- Workers focused on a single task will find better ways to improve efficiency.

WHEN TO BULLSHIT
- When you want to bullshit your coworkers into doing your work for you, use specialization and division of labor (i.e., break up the work so that you utilize each person's strengths and get the work done faster).

THE STOCK MARKET
When to buy and when to sell.

HOW IT WORKS
- The stock market raises capital so a company can continue producing its good or service.
- A person invests in a stock or share of money in a particular company.
- If the company does well, the shares increase in value.
- If the company loses value, so, too, does the stock.

TERMINOLOGY
- P/E Ratio—the price per earnings ratio shows how much money companies earn relative to the price of their shares.
- Diversification—do not invest in one thing alone. Spread the wealth so that if one stock fails, you still have others.
- The Dow Jones—the average share price of the thirty most powerful stocks on the New York Stock Exchange. It is viewed as an indication of how the U.S. economy is performing.

HOW TO INVEST
- Buy when stocks are low and sell when stocks are high.
- Patience is a virtue in the stock market. Do not take your share out when it is low. Over time, it will rise.
- Remember to diversify your investments.

INFORMATION TO USE WHEN BULLSHITTING
- A bull market is when the stock market is improving and investors believe it will continue this way.
- A bull market is characterized by a twenty percent increase in prices, shares traded, and number of companies entering the stock market.
- A bear market is the opposite of a bull market, when value decreases by twenty percent.

WHEN TO BULLSHIT
- When investing and getting information from others about good investments.

REAGANOMICS
Love it or hate it, here's what you need to know about it.
AKA Supply-side economics.

WHAT IT IS
- The controversial economic program begun in Ronald Reagan's presidency.

- The notion that decreasing taxes for businesses and investors will increase revenues, and as a result, there will be a trickle-down effect.
- There were four major guidelines:
  1. Reduce government spending.
  2. Reduce marginal tax rates (both income and capital).
  3. Reduce regulation.
  4. Reduce inflation by controlling money supply.

PRAISE

- The policy gained praise for its notion that it would limit the role of government and increase consumer spending.
- It was also praised for decreasing unemployment and interest rates.

CRITICISM

- The policy gained a considerable amount of criticism because of the trickle-down aspect of the program.
- Though income for the wealthy and middle class improved, the standard of living for the lower class, and in particular minorities, declined as tax rates increased.

IMPACT

- Many industries were deregulated and government spending was cut in welfare and education.

WHEN TO BULLSHIT

- When discussing politics and economics.
- When taking a side as to whether Reaganomics is a good—or bad—thing.

GAME THEORY

Determining company strategies.

WHAT IT IS

- Applied mathematics relating to the prediction of behavior and strategy.

- Useful in understanding why companies make their decisions and how those decisions will affect others.

HOW IT WORKS
- Game theory uses complex mathematic formulas, algorithms, and matrices to determine the best strategy for success.
- It does so by predicting the most plausible actions the "opponent" might make.

HOW IT WORKS IN THE MARKETPLACE
- Game theorists analyze companies and market trends and try to determine probable decisions companies will make, and what direction the market will go.

TERMS
- Game—result of circumstances from the actions of two or more players, or decision makers.
- Strategy—the plan of action each player will take as circumstances arise.
- Equilibrium—the point where all players involved have reached their decisions and the result is in.

NASH EQUILIBRIUM
- Though not his original idea, the contributions made by John Nash (of *A Beautiful Mind*) to game theory won him a Nobel Prize in Economics.
- The simple idea behind a Nash equilibrium is when players competing against one another follow their optimum strategy to succeed regardless of the actions of the other player involved.

WHEN TO BULLSHIT
- When watching *A Beautiful Mind*, you can provide some insight into just how important Nash's work really was.
- When playing a board game, remind your opponents they could be playing a game that's far more complicated.

MARXISM
The importance of the working class (and communism).

WHAT IT IS
- The economic and political theories of Karl Marx.
- One of Marx's major works was *Capital: A Critique of Political Economy*.
- Marxism became the foundation for communism.
- Marxism claims that capitalism exploits the worker, and that the true, utopian economic system is communism.

LABOR THEORY OF VALUE
- The value of a good or service can be measured by the average amount of hours required to create the good or service.
- Marx argues that capitalists do not pay workers the complete value of the goods they produce, but instead pay only what is necessary to ensure that he continues working.
- Surplus value is the difference between the worker's value and how much the worker gets paid.

ALIENATION
- Marx claimed capitalism alienates the workers because even though they are the ones producing goods, the market forces control them.
- Marx claimed as long as society was run by private property and competition, people will be alienated.

COMMUNISM
- Marxism claims communism will provide more freedom to the working class, with wealth redistributed to everyone.

THE REALITY OF MARXISM
- When applied in the real world, Marxism has failed.
- Communism has created widespread poverty and political dictators, while capitalism has created and promoted economic growth.

LAISSEZ-FAIRE

Making sense of market forces.

WHAT IT IS
- Claims that market forces should drive the economic system and it should not include intervention or moderation from the government.
- Laissez-faire came from Adam Smith, the eighteenth-century Scot who is credited as being the founder of modern economics.
- Laissez-faire is one of the main principles of capitalism.
- In contrast to laissez-faire is Keynesian economics, which claims government intervention is best for the economy and ensures a stable growth.

BACKLASH AGAINST LAISSEZ-FAIRE
- The mid-nineteenth and early twentieth centuries saw the rise of monopolies, disregard for worker and consumer safety, and a great disproportion in the distribution of wealth.
- Woodrow Wilson's "the new freedom" sought to regulate the banks, revise the tariff, and modify antitrust laws.

RETURN OF LAISSEZ-FAIRE
- In the 1970s, laissez-faire economics (now called free-market economics) returned when the government attempted to deregulate industries such as transportation, promoting independent competition and pricing among service providers.

Chapter 12

Science— Lab Rats, Test Tubes, and Far-Out Theories

BIOLOGY

The breakdown of life.

WHAT IT IS

- Biology is the study of life.

THE MAJOR PRINCIPLES OF BIOLOGY

1. Cells are the basic unit of every living thing.
2. Living things use and transform energy.
3. Species continue to thrive through reproduction.
4. Over a lifetime, living things grow.
5. Genes are the hereditary units in every living thing.
6. Evolution is responsible for the variation in species and traits.

7. Living beings regulate and maintain homeostasis, or a stable, internal condition.

GREGOR MENDEL AND HEREDITY

- In studying pea plants, Gregor Mendel, a nineteenth-century Austrian monk, discovered the foundation of heredity.
- The law of segregation—during the production of sexually reproductive cells, or gametes, the gene's copies separate and each gamete is given one copy. The offspring will receive one hereditary factor from each parent.
- The law of independent assortment—characteristics are transmitted to the offspring randomly because different versions of a gene separate independently.

EVOLUTION

- Based on Charles Darwin's On the *Origin of Species*.
- Species have evolved over time through natural selection. Organisms with the most desirable and beneficial traits have survived, and these genetic traits are passed down to offspring.

WHEN TO BULLSHIT

- When at the zoo—sound so believable she thinks she's with a zoologist.

CHEMISTRY

When chemicals react.

WHAT IT IS

- Chemistry is the study of chemical interactions.
- Chemistry encompasses all of the natural sciences (biology, physics, astronomy, and geology).

KEY CONCEPTS

- Atoms are the basic unit of all forms of matter. They consist of a positively charged nucleus and negatively charged electrons.
- An element is a substance that is made from the same type of atoms.

- A compound is a substance with a certain ratio of elements.
- A molecule is the smallest unit of a compound.
- When atoms stick together, they form a bond between the positive and negative charges.
- Chemicals exist in phases: solid, liquid, and gas.
- Substances can be classified as acidic or basic.
- Acids produce hydronium ions when the substance is dissolved in water.
- Bases produce hydroxide ions when the substance is dissolved in water.

THE PERIODIC TABLE
- The periodic table is a reference of all known elements.
- There are currently 118 elements.

INFORMATION TO USE WHEN BULLSHITTING
- Oxygen as a gas is colorless; however, when it is a solid or liquid, it's blue.
- Helium is lighter than air; this is the reason helium balloons rise.
- "J" is the only letter that does not appear on the periodic table.

WHEN TO BULLSHIT
- Don't just blow things up for the sake of blowing things up; sound scientific about the process.

PHYSICS
Gravity and all that good stuff.

WHAT IT IS
- Physics is the study of matter, energy, time, and the interactions between them.
- Physics ranges from microscopic particles to the study of galaxies.

NEWTON'S LAW OF UNIVERSAL GRAVITATION
- All objects in the universe have a gravitational pull towards one another, and the force is universal.

EINSTEIN'S THEORY OF RELATIVITY

- Established by Albert Einstein in 1915, it can be broken up into two parts.
  - The special theory of relativity states the laws of physics are the same at rest as they are in a uniformly moving room.
  - The general theory of relativity expands on Newton's theory that gravity works in open space, and shows that objects move in a straight line in space and time.

STRING THEORY

- String Theory attempts to explain gravity, electromagnetic force, strong nuclear force (what holds atoms together), and weak nuclear force.
- Elementary particles are superstrings, or tiny loops of energy that vibrate.
- The properties of the string come from the vibration.
- The more frantic the vibration, the more energy is created (which means more mass is created because mass is equal to energy).
- In order to work, strings must vibrate in ten-dimensional space (of which we only see four: height, width, depth, and time).

WHEN TO BULLSHIT
- When you want to sound extremely, extremely intelligent.

ASTRONOMY
(Big) Bang it out of the park.

WHAT IT IS
- The study of celestial objects and the formation of the universe.

THE BIG BANG
- The big bang theory is generally accepted as an explanation of how the universe began.
- It started out extremely hot, and fourteen billion years ago, began to cool and expand.

- The cooling allowed atoms to form and cluster, building the stars and galaxy.
- There is still great debate as to what caused the big bang and what happened in the moments after.

SUPERNOVAS
- A supernova occurs when a star has reached the end of its life and explodes.
- Not all stars turn into supernovas; it depends on their mass.
- There are two types of supernovas:
  1. Type I—a star accumulates matter from its neighboring mass until a reaction is ignited.
  2. Type II—a star internally collapses. To have a Type II supernova, there must be the presence of hydrogen in the spectrum, and the mass of the star must be nine times that of the sun.

DARK MATTER
- An invisible matter believed to make up 90 percent of the universe.
- Dark matter can only be observed by the gravitational forces exerted.

WHEN TO BULLSHIT
- Impress your friends around the campfire as you stargaze.
- When wanting to sound intelligent.

ECOLOGY
A matter of class.

WHAT IT IS
- The study of organisms and their interactions in their natural environment.
- Ecology also determines the abundance and distribution of organisms.

TERMS
- Population—a group of a single type of organism that lives in an area.

- Community—all of the populations living in a certain area.
- Ecosystem—the community interacting with the nonliving environment.
- Biosphere—all of the ecosystems combined.
- Genus—groups of organisms of the same species.

ABIOTIC AND BIOTIC FACTORS

- Abiotic factors are non-living factors that affect organisms in a biosphere such as temperature, light, soil, and water.
- Biotic factors are the living parts within the ecosystem with which organisms interact. An example of a biotic factor would be predation.

COEVOLUTION

- Mutualism—when both organisms benefit from a relationship.
  - For example, bees need flowers for their pollen, and flowers need bees to spread their pollen.
- Commensalism—when one organism benefits and the other organism isn't affected.
  - For example, barnacles adhere to the skin of whales for nutrients, but their presence does not affect the whale.
- Parasitism—when one organism benefits while harming the other organism.
  - For example, tapeworms eat the nutrients a human consumes, and in return, the human will get sick.

WHEN TO BULLSHIT
- When trying to bullshit your colleagues, compare your relationship to the various forms of coevolution (maybe leaving out parasitism).

GEOLOGY
Rocks rock!

WHAT IT IS
- The study of the rocks, minerals, and liquids that make up the earth, and the processes that have shaped and changed how the earth is today.

ROCKS AND MINERALS

- There are three types of rocks.
  - Igneous—when lava or magma cools down and turns into a solid.
  - Sedentary—rocks formed by erosion and weathering of sediment.
  - Metamorphic—the resulting transformation of other rocks through heat or pressure.
- A mineral is the building block of a rock. It is a solid chemical substance that is formed naturally.

GEOLOGIC PROCESSES

- Erosion—the processes that break down the rocks and carry the products away.
- Mechanical weathering—disintegration of rock into smaller parts.
- Chemical weathering—when the original material transforms into a substance with different physical characteristics and composition.

GEOLOGIC TIME PERIODS

- Phanerozoic Eon—the emergence of plant and wildlife. During this time, the continents formed into a single landmass known as Pangaea, and then separated into the continents we have today.
- Proterozoic Eon—during this time, the planet evolved into an oxygenated atmosphere.
- Archean Eon—there was a lack of free oxygen in the atmosphere, and only single-celled life forms existed.

WHEN TO BULLSHIT
- When trying to impress someone while taking a hike.

MICROBIOLOGY

Making the world around you smaller and smaller.

WHAT IT IS
- Microbiology is the study of microorganisms, or microbes, and how they interact with their environment.

- This includes single-celled organisms, bacteria, fungi, and viruses (even though viruses are not classified as living organisms).

SOME FIELDS OF MICROBIOLOGY

- There are many fields within microbiology because microorganisms impact all aspects of the environment.
  - Immunology—study of the immune system, in particular, how the body protects itself from infection.
  - Epidemiology—monitoring the spread of disease within communities.
  - Agricultural Microbiology—focuses on the relationship between microbes and plant life, with particular concentration on fighting plant diseases and increasing the yield of crops.
  - Food Microbiology—studying foodborne illnesses and the causes of spoilage. Food microbiology also uses microorganisms to produce food in methods such as fermentation.
  - Genetic Engineering—altering of the genetic makeup of organisms to produce drugs and hormones.

BENEFITS OF MICROBIOLOGY

- Microbiology is responsible for the creation of pesticides, vaccinations, antibiotics, hormones, and even food.

WHEN TO BULLSHIT
- When trying to convince your coworkers to go over every little detail.

ANTHROPOLOGY
What it means to be human.

WHAT IT IS
- The study of human beings, both past and present.
- Studies not only the biological and physical aspects of humans, but the social as well.

CULTURAL ANTHROPOLOGY
- Anthropology studies living people.
- It focuses on beliefs, technologies, values, practices, and social, or political trends.
- The field looks at the similarities and differences among societies in issues regarding race, sexuality, class, and nationality.

LINGUISTIC ANTHROPOLOGY
- Linguistic anthropology studies human languages and the practice of speaking.
- It examines the role language plays in establishing control, belief systems, and ideologies.

PHYSICAL ANTHROPOLOGY
- It studies the biological makeup of humans and their ancestors.
- It looks at the evolution of humans and how they adapted to particular environments.
- To understand the people of the past, physical anthropologists study the fossil record, artifacts, primates, and genetics of people living today.

WHEN TO BULLSHIT
- When referring to yourself as a real "people person."

PALEONTOLOGY
When the once living leave behind a part of themselves.

WHAT IT IS
- It is the study of the ancient life that once inhabited the earth.
- Paleontology uses fossils to determine the conditions of the earth during the lifetime of the organisms.
- Many people associate paleontology with the study of dinosaurs, but there are many fields within paleontology, including the study of ancient plant life, invertebrates, and primitive humans.

- Paleontology uses historical evidence to conclude findings rather than conduct experiments.

WHAT ARE FOSSILS
- Fossils are the preserved remains of an organism.

INFORMATION TO USE WHEN BULLSHITTING
- The La Brea Tar Pits, located in the heart of Los Angeles, California, are a paleontology goldmine.
- Animals approached the pits thinking it was a watering hole and got stuck in the tar.
- These trapped animals would entice predators such as a saber-tooth cat to come, thinking it had a free meal.
- When the predator killed the animal, it soon became trapped in the tar as well.
- Inside the pits are over three billion prehistoric creatures, including mammoths, saber-tooth cats, dire wolves, and giant sloths.

WHEN TO BULLSHIT
- When attending a museum.
- When trying to impress someone as you watch *Jurassic Park*.

ARCHAEOLOGY
Mankind (and all kinds of man).

WHAT IT IS
- Archaeology is the study of past humans and the societies they lived in.
- Archaeology is a form of anthropology.

TERMS
- Hominid is a family of bipedal and erect primates.
- Homo is the genus of hominids that includes modern humans and their ancestors.

THE FIRST HUMANS

- Archaeologists believe humans' ancestors first split from chimpanzees five to seven million years ago.
- Homo habilis is believed to be the first ancestor of modern humans, or Homo sapiens. H. habilis is believed to have lived one to two million years ago.
- Homo erectus lived over one million years ago, replacing H. habilis, and is the first hominid to migrate and distribute across the Old World.
- Homo sapiens came into existence 300,000 years ago. Fully modern humans were in existence 100,000 years ago.

NEANDERTHALS

- 30,000 to 400,000 years ago, during the time of Homo sapiens, another species existed called Homo neanderthalensis.
- Scientists believe H. sapien and H. neanderthalensis shared a common ancestor around 600,000 years ago.
- They also believe that not only did Neanderthals coexist with Homo sapiens but the two species interbred around 75,000 years ago.
- There are two theories as to why the species went extinct:
  - Competition and conflict with Homo sapiens.
  - The species disappeared through absorption as a result of interbreeding with H. sapiens.

INFORMATION TO USE WHEN BULLSHITTING

- Scientists have discovered that Europeans and Asians have one to four percent of Neanderthal DNA in their genetic makeup.

WHEN TO BULLSHIT

- When visiting a museum you can explain why your forehead is the same shape as the mannequin Neanderthal's.

Chapter 13

History— Get Enlightened

ANCIENT EGYPT

From the Pyramids to Tutankhamen.

THE EARLY DYNASTIC PERIOD (3050–2686 B.C.)

- King Menes is considered the founder of the first Dynasty and responsible for uniting the two halves of Egypt: the upper and lower parts.

THE OLD KINGDOM (2686–2181 B.C.)

- Known as the "age of the pyramids," twenty major pyramids were constructed during this time.

FIRST INTERMEDIATE PERIOD (2181–2040 B.C.)

- Conflict between the upper and lower halves of Egypt makes the central government collapse.

THE MIDDLE KINGDOM (2040–1782 B.C.)

- The conflict ends and Egypt sees a resurgence and change in art, literature, and religion.
- Amenemhat I comes to power and expands trade.

THE SECOND INTERMEDIATE PERIOD (1782–1570 B.C.)

- For almost 100 years, Egypt is ruled by foreign emperors and the weak country is taken advantage of by Hyksos from Asia.

THE NEW KINGDOM (1540–1090 B.C.)

- The Egyptians drive the Hyksos out of their kingdom.
- Amenhotep IV becomes king and decides to turn the polytheistic religion into a monotheistic one.
- Tutankhamen comes to power, returning the country to a polytheistic religion.
- The later part of the New Kingdom is considered to be the "golden age" of Egypt, with the empire regaining its land in Asia.

WHEN TO BULLSHIT

- When dressing like an authentic mummy for Halloween.
- When traveling to Egypt and impressing everyone around you.
- When trying to sound cultured.
- When expressing to your coworkers which Pharaoh you think your boss most likely represents.

ANCIENT ROME

When in Rome . . . the Romans did a lot.

THE LEGEND OF ROME'S ORIGINS

- Romulus and Remus, the children of the god, Mars, were raised by a she-wolf, until ultimately being found by a shepherd and his wife. When the boys grew older, they decided to build a city. In a fight over who should rule the city, Romulus kills Remus with a rock and names the city after himself.

THE ROMAN KINGDOM (753–509 B.C.)

- The Roman Kingdom is established by the Tiber River and is ruled by seven kings who are elected to serve for life.
- The Kingdom grows, expanding 350 square miles.

THE ROMAN REPUBLIC (500–30 B.C.)

- After overthrowing the last king, Rome is ruled by an aristocratic government, with a focus on separation of powers and a system of checks and balances in place.
- During the Republic, Rome expands throughout the Mediterranean, and into North Africa, Greece, and the Iberian Peninsula.
- In 60 B.C., Julius Caesar comes to power after a civil war.
- When Caesar is assassinated in 44 B.C., Octavian, Mark Antony, and Lepidus take power. Octavian comes to strip Lepidus of his powers and defeat Mark Antony in 31 B.C., becoming the sole ruler.

THE ROMAN EMPIRE (27 B.C.–A.D. 1453)

- Octavian changes his name to Augustus and takes complete control of empire, leaving the republican government intact.
- Under Trajan, the Roman Empire expands 6.5 million square kilometers.
- To better control such a large empire, authority is divided among four co-emperors.
- Over time, these divisions will separate the Western Empire from the Eastern Empire.
- The Western Empire collapses in 476, and the Eastern Empire collapses in 1453.

WHEN TO BULLSHIT
- After watching *Gladiator*, you can discuss the film and the time period.
- When watching *Roman Holiday*, pick out which character you think would make the best Octavian.

THE RENAISSANCE

Relive a classic.
WHEN: 1450–1600

WHAT IT WAS

- The Renaissance was a cultural movement originating in Italy that spanned across Europe.

- The time period is defined by innovations in the arts, politics, philosophy, literature, religion, and science.

ITALIAN RENAISSANCE
- The Early Renaissance begins in Florence, Italy, with much of the work commissioned by the Medici family.
- The Late Renaissance centers around Rome, with much of the work commissioned by the Popes.
- The Italian Renaissance is notable for its return to classical art and philosophy, and advancement in painting and sculpture.
- The Italian Renaissance sees a rise of a wealthy merchant class, allowing for more art to be made.

NORTHERN RENAISSANCE
- Influences of the Italian Renaissance spread throughout Europe.
- With disenchantment with the Church increasing, the Northern Renaissance paves the way for the Protestant Reformation.
- In England, the dominant art form is not painting but literature, and the most prominent figures to come from this time are William Shakespeare and John Milton.

TECHNOLOGICAL ADVANCES
- There were many technological advances during the Renaissance that influenced the work of this time period greatly. These include the printing press, the microscope, and the submarine.

WHEN TO BULLSHIT
- When referring to yourself as a "Renaissance man," back it up with some knowledge of the time.

FRENCH REVOLUTION

Vive la Revolution!
WHEN: 1789–1799

CAUSES
- The American Revolution brings ideas of democracy.
- Because of the wars France takes part in, the nation's money supply is diminishing and there is famine, especially a lack of bread.
- People start questioning the divine right of King Louis XVI, the idea that he has been picked by God to rule the country.
- France practices a class system known as the Three Estates, in which the higher classes are given special privileges (such as not paying taxes).
- At a time of great debt, King Louis XVI refuses to make changes to the system.

SOME MAJOR EVENTS
- The Tennis Court Oath—The Third Estate, representing the underprivileged class, forms a national assembly. Locked out of their meeting hall, they move to a nearby tennis court and take an oath never to separate until a constitution is made in France.
- The Storming of the Bastille—The Bastille, a royal prison and symbol of oppression, is overtaken by hundreds of angry French citizens. After gunfire, the governor of the Bastille surrenders. He is beheaded and his head is put on a stake.
- The Third Estate creates a constitution, and King Louis XVI is caught trying to escape.
- King Louis XVI is beheaded, and a new republic is formed under Napoleon Bonaparte.

WHEN TO BULLSHIT
- When out with a date, bring some history into your French meal (and enjoy the bread).

REVOLUTIONARY WAR

A lot of tea ended up in the harbor.
WHEN: 1775–1783

WHO FOUGHT

- The thirteen colonies versus Great Britain.

WHAT LED TO THE WAR

- As Great Britain continually imposes taxes (The Sugar Act of 1764, The Stamp Act of 1765, The Townshend Acts of 1767) on the colonists without representation, tensions start growing.
- The Boston Massacre takes place on March 5, 1770.
- Five American colonists are killed by British troops.
- The Boston Tea Party takes place on December 16, 1773.
- As a result of Great Britain's imposing a new tax on tea, a group of Americans dress up as Native Americans and dump 342 crates of tea from Britain into Boston harbor.
- The Continental Congress takes place in 1774 and 1775.
- The colonies gather together to discuss their liberty. From the discussions during the second meeting comes the Declaration of Independence.

SOME MAJOR EVENTS

- April 18, 1775, Paul Revere rides on his horse warning of the British attack.
- April 19, 1775, The Battles of Lexington and Concord are the first battles fought.
- July 4, 1776, the Declaration of Independence is adopted.
- December 26, 1776, Washington surprise attacks the British in the Battle of Trenton.
- October 20, 1781, the British surrender at the Battle of Yorktown, ending the war.

WHEN TO BULLSHIT
- When trying to sound like a war buff.
- When trying to impress your date as you walk along the Freedom Trail in Boston.
- When persuading your friends to partake in a war re-enactment.

INDUSTRIAL REVOLUTION
Machines make headlines.

WHAT IT WAS
- Technological developments changed the world from an agricultural economy to an industrial one.

THE FIRST INDUSTRIAL REVOLUTION (1750–1850)
- Beginning in England, the industrial revolution begins with the introduction of textile manufacturing and the steam engine.

THE SECOND INDUSTRIAL REVOLUTION (1850–1940)
- The second industrial revolution takes place in the United States with the introduction of electricity and the internal combustion engine.

SOME IMPORTANT INVENTIONS
- The steam engine and steam power are developed.
- Steam engines are applied to steamboats all over the United States, and are instrumental in making transportation of goods faster.
- Steam power begins to be used in factories and industrial machinery.
- In 1793, Eli Whitney, an American from the Northeast, is living on a southern plantation. He creates the cotton gin to remove seeds from the cotton.
- The cotton gin will revolutionize the cotton industry, cleaning up to fifty pounds of cotton a day.
- As a result of the cotton gin, the United States begins growing three-quarters of the world's cotton supply and develops the textile industry.

RESULTS OF INDUSTRIAL REVOLUTION
- The industrial revolution creates the factory system and the notion of the assembly line.
- With the rise of industry, people move away from farms and into cities.
- New social classes arise, including the emerging middle class.

WHEN TO BULLSHIT
- When discussing the advancements of technology today, you can dive deep into history for your bullshit. "Sure, that phone can play a game, but have you ever heard of the cotton gin?"

CIVIL WAR
A nation divided.
WHEN: 1861–1865

WHO FOUGHT
- United States of America (Union) versus Confederate States of America (Confederacy).

WHAT IT WAS
- Eleven southern slave states declare secession from the United States.
- Led by Jefferson Davis, they form the Confederate States of America, and, citing frustrations with such issues as taxation, states' rights, and slavery, begin a war with the United States.

MAJOR BATTLES
- April 12–13, 1861, Battle of Fort Sumter—the battle that begins the Civil War. Upon their secession from the Union, South Carolina demands that the U. S. Army forfeit control of Fort Sumter in Charleston Harbor. When the Union refuses, the Confederate army leads an attack that lasts through the night. The Union withdraws the next day and Confederate forces take control of the Fort.
- September 17, 1862, Battle of Antietam—first major battle fought on northern soil and the bloodiest single-day battle in American history.

General Robert E. Lee leads the Confederates and Major General George B. McClellan leads the Union forces. Though there is no conclusive winner, the battle remains significant because President Abraham Lincoln thinks it enough of a victory to announce the Emancipation Proclamation.

WINNER
- The Union.

DEATH TOLL
- 1,030,000, including 620,000 soldiers.
- The Civil War is considered the deadliest war in American history.

CONSEQUENCES
- Ends slavery for the Confederacy's 3.5 million blacks.

WHEN TO BULLSHIT
- When standing in front of the Lincoln Memorial you can provide a history lesson.

THE GREAT DEPRESSION
The Stock Market crashes—hard.
WHEN: 1929–1939

WHAT IT WAS
- A worldwide economic depression.

WHAT HAPPENED
- Prior to the crash, the stock market had been rising and had become increasingly popular, with many believing it to be a quick way to get rich.
- People bought stocks "on margin," meaning, even though they didn't have enough to pay for a stock, they would put ten to twenty percent down and a broker would pay for the rest.
- Companies began putting money into the stock market, and even banks put their customer's money in the market.

- On October 24, 1929, known as Black Thursday, the stock market crashes and prices plummet; margin calls are sent to people (the person has to pay the broker the cost of the loan).
- October 29, 1929, or Black Tuesday, is known as the worst day in the history of the stock market. Prices of stocks collapse as everyone wants to sell and no one wants to buy.
- Because of the United States' role in financially aiding other countries after WWI, the depression spreads through Europe.

THE NEW DEAL

- In 1932, Franklin D. Roosevelt becomes president, and his plan for economic recovery is known as the New Deal.
- The New Deal establishes a series of programs to create job opportunities.

THE END OF THE GREAT DEPRESSION

- The economy improves over the years, but it is only when the United States enters World War II that the Great Depression truly ends.

WHEN TO BULLSHIT

- When comparing the Great Depression to today's current recession.

WORLD WAR I

The power of alliances.
WHEN: 1914–1918

WHO FOUGHT: THE ALLIES VERSUS THE CENTRAL POWERS

THE ALLIES

- The United Kingdom, Russia, and France are originally known as the Triple Entente.
- Later the United States would join.
- Though other countries would join, these are the major four powers.

THE CENTRAL POWERS

- Germany, Austria-Hungary, and Turkey are the three major forces behind the Central Powers.
- Italy begins as a Central Power, but switches to the Allies.

CAUSES OF THE WAR

- Alliances formed between countries at the end of the Franco-Prussian War, splitting the continent.
- The rise of nationalism, militarism, and imperialism creates tensions among nations.

MAJOR EVENTS

- August 14, 1914, Franz Ferdinand, the Archduke of Austria-Hungary, is assassinated. Austria-Hungary declares war on Serbia, and because of the alliances, many countries enter into the conflict.
- In 1915, the Allies attack the Ottoman Empire.
- 1916 and 1917 are dominated by trench warfare.
- In April 1917, the United States declares war on Germany after the sinking of the *Lusitania*, a British transport and cruise ship heading to New York.
- In November 1917, Russia pulls out of the war as a result of the Bolshevik Revolution.
- As fighting continues, the Central Powers grow weaker, and eventually, all sign armistice agreements.
- The Treaty of Versailles makes Germany take responsibility for the war and pay reparations. It also redistributes the German empire, and restricts its military powers.

WHEN TO BULLSHIT

- When talking about European relations and making a link to WWII.
- When discussing wars and history with people.

WORLD WAR II

Hitler rises to power and the whole world goes to war.
WHEN: 1939–1945

CAUSES

- Growing resentment of the Treaty of Versailles by Germany and the rise of Adolf Hitler and the Nazi regime.
- The Great Depression.
- A failing League of Nations.

MAIN EVENTS

- In September 1939, Germany invades Poland. In response, France and Britain declare war on Germany. That same year, Japan enters into an alliance with Italy and Germany.
- In 1940, Germany conquers Belgium, Norway, the Netherlands, and France. Germany attempts to conquer Britain but fails.
- In 1941, Germany invades the Soviet Union. Though the invasion is successful, the land is far too massive and the winters too cold for the Germans to succeed. Germany retreats in 1943.
- The Holocaust, Nazi Germany's mass genocide of the Jewish people, will claim six million lives through executions and concentration camps.
- On December 7, 1941, Japan launches a surprise attack on the U.S. Navy base, Pearl Harbor, bringing America into the war.
- On June 6, 1944, American and British troops land on the beaches of Normandy on what is known as D-Day. On August 25, Paris is liberated.
- In 1945, Russia invades Germany from the east as the Allies proceed from the west. Hitler commits suicide and Germany surrenders on May 8, otherwise known as V-E Day.
- In 1945, the United States drops two atomic bombs on Japan. Japan surrenders and the war ends.

WHEN TO BULLSHIT

- When talking with a veteran or history buff.
- When traveling to Europe you can show previous knowledge of any sites you visit.

CIVIL-RIGHTS MOVEMENT

Freedom at last.
WHEN: 1955–1968

WHAT IT WAS

- The quality of life for African Americans was anything but equal while living under the Jim Crow laws in the South. During the latter part of the twentieth century, African Americans stood up for their rights.

KEY EVENTS

- 1954: *Brown v. Board of Education*.
  - Linda Brown, a black girl in the third grade, had to walk a mile to get to her elementary school when a white school was much closer to where she lived. When asked by her father if she could attend the school, the principal denied her access.
  - When the case goes to the Supreme Court, the Justices rule that segregation of children in schools based solely on race is unequal.
- On December 1, 1955, Rosa Parks refuses to give her seat up on the bus to a white passenger.
  - In response to Park's arrest, African Americans boycott Montgomery buses for 381 days, reducing revenue by 80 percent.
- The March on Washington takes place in March 1963.
  - Among other things, civil-rights organizations march for the right to vote, an end to segregated education, and passage of civil-rights legislation.
  - Around 300,000 demonstrators gather at Lincoln Memorial.
  - Martin Luther delivers his famous "I Have a Dream" speech.
- Civil-Rights Act of 1964 passes.
  - It bans discrimination in schools and public accommodations.

PROMINENT FIGURES

- Martin Luther King, Jr.—believed in peaceful, nonviolent demonstrations
- Malcolm X—rejected the notion of nonviolent protests and urged the black population to rise up
- W. E. B. Du Bois—became one of the founders of the National Association for the Advancement of Colored People (NAACP)

COLD WAR

Uncle Sam versus Mother Russia.
WHEN: 1945–1980

WHO IT INVOLVED
- The United States of America
- The Soviet Union

WHAT IT WAS
- The Cold War was a conflict between the communist ideology of the Soviet Union and the democratic and capitalist ideals of the United States.
- As the Soviet Union expanded into Eastern Europe, the threat of communism became evermore present to the United States.
- Tensions rose with the advent of nuclear weapons, which both sides had and threatened to use.

MCCARTHYISM
- In the late 1940s to 1950s, Wisconsin Senator Joe McCarthy leads the House Un-American Activities Committee (HUAC) in investigating communist organizations in the United States.
- McCarthy sees entertainment as brainwashing the population, and holds unfair hearings for many people in the entertainment industry including actors, writers, and artists. Even civil-rights activists are subject to hearings.
- Many are blacklisted as a result of the hearings, and their careers are destroyed because people fear working with them.

CUBAN MISSILE CRISIS

- In 1962, the Soviet Union begins placing intermediate-range missiles in Cuba.
- Upon finding out, President Kennedy deploys a naval quarantine around Cuba, and makes it clear to the public that should Cuba launch any missiles, it will mean war between the United States and the Soviet Union.
- Tensions continue to rise until finally, the Soviet Union Premier agrees to remove the missiles if the United States does not attack Cuba and removes some of its missiles in Turkey.
- Many believe that the Cuban Missile Crisis is the closest we have ever come to a nuclear war.

THE END OF THE WAR

- In the 1980s, the Soviet Union is fighting a war in Afghanistan, is involved in a pricey arms race, and faces a faltering economy.
- When the Berlin wall comes down, communist regimes in Eastern Europe are ousted in free elections and in 1991, the Soviet Union dissolves.

INFORMATION TO USE WHEN BULLSHITTING

- HUAC even goes so far as to question actress Shirley Temple, who was ten years old at the time.
- One of the major causes of the Cuban Missile Crisis is the Bay of Pigs, the United States' very public but failed attempt at taking down Cuban Premier Fidel Castro.

WHEN TO BULLSHIT

- When discussing the impact communism has on the nation and explaining how you're glad you're not living during that time.

THE SPACE RACE

Taking the Cold War tensions to another level.
WHEN: The 1950s and 1960s

WHAT IT WAS

- In the midst of the Cold War, the tensions between the United States and the Soviet Union turn to a new direction: outer space.
- As the Soviet Union begins advancing in technology, America, then considered the leader in technology, views this as a threat.

SPUTNIK 1

- On October 4, 1957, the Soviet Union launches the world's first artificial satellite, Sputnik 1.
- Sputnik 1 creates great havoc among the U.S. population, many fearing it is a weapon or bomb.
- Four months after Sputnik 1, the United States launches Explorer 1.

THE SOVIET UNION LEADS

- On April 12, 1961, the Soviet Union's Yuri Gagarin becomes the first man to enter orbit.
- Twenty-three days later, the Americans have their first man enter orbit.
- On June 16, 1963, the Soviet Union sends the first woman into orbit.

AMERICA IS TRIUMPHANT

- In 1961, fearing the Soviet Union will win the space race, President John F. Kennedy tells NASA his plan of sending a man to the moon.
- On July 20, 1969, eight years after Kennedy announced his plan, Neil Armstrong from the Apollo 11 mission becomes the first man on the moon.
- The Space Race does not officially end until the disintegration of the Soviet Union.

WHEN TO BULLSHIT

- When discussing space programs of the past and present day.

MODERN WARS
Keeping up with the times.

THE WAR ON TERROR
- On September 11, 2001, four commercial airplanes were hijacked by 19 members of the militant Islamic group, al-Qaeda. Two planes were flown into the Twin Towers of the World Trade Center in New York City, one plane was flown into the Pentagon, and the last plane, targeted for the White House, crashed in Pennsylvania as a result of passengers onboard attempting to retake the plane.
- On September 20th, President George Bush coined the phrase "War on Terror." The objectives were to defeat terrorists and their organizations, eliminate terrorist support, sponsorship, and sanctuary, and to protect the interests of the United States and citizens, both at home and abroad.
- Upon taking office, President Barack Obama has not used the phrase.

THE IRAQ WAR
- On March 19, 2003, President Bush launched the invasion of Iraq in search for weapons of mass destruction.
- On December 14, 2003, Saddam Hussein was captured.
- The Iraqi Interim Government, created by the United States and allies, came to power on June 28, 2004, and elections were scheduled for January of 2005.
- On November 5, 2006, Saddam Hussein was found guilty for the 1982 killing of 148 Shiites and was sentenced to death by hanging.
- No weapons of mass destruction were ever found in Iraq, and the 9-11 Commission declared there was no collaboration between Hussein and al-Qaeda.
- On August 19, 2010, the last of the U.S. combat brigades left Iraq.

AFGHANISTAN
- Began on October 7, 2001, with the launch of Operation Enduring Freedom in an effort to defeat al-Qaeda.
- The Taliban regime was ousted from Kabul, and in its place an interim government came into power under Hamid Karzai.

- The Taliban, now working from Pakistan, have made a series of insurgent attacks in Afghanistan.
- On December 1, 2009, President Obama announced 30,000 more troops would be sent to Afghanistan over six months and set a withdrawal date for 2014.

WHEN TO BULLSHIT
- Be able to discuss current events or politics without sounding clueless.

Chapter 14

Politics— Everyone's a Pundit

DEMOCRACY
By the people, for the people.

WHAT IT IS
- The word democracy comes from the Greek demos, meaning people.
- In a democracy, the people make legislative decisions.

FORMS OF DEMOCRACY
- Direct democracy—citizens make decisions regarding the policies and laws directly.
- Direct democracy originated in Athens, Greece, in the fifth century B.C.
- Athenian men over the age of eighteen were the only ones allowed to vote.
- Representative democracy—citizens vote for representatives to govern.
- This is the model of democracy used by the United States.
- A democratic republic is a form of representative democracy where the people also elect the head of state.

- Parliamentary democracy—a form of representative democracy where the dominant party within the legislature selects the members of government.
- Countries with a parliamentary democracy include the Czech Republic, Hungary, and Israel.

WHEN TO BULLSHIT
- When caught in a political debate you need to bullshit your way out of.

COMMUNISM
All aspects of life run by the government.

WHAT IT IS
- Communism is a political and economic philosophy based on *The Communist Manifesto* by Karl Marx, and *Principles of Communism* by Friedrich Engels.
- Communism calls for an abolition of capitalism, private ownership, and private profit.
- It is based on government control of labor, education, communication, transport, agriculture, and factories, as well as an abolition of religion and the class system.
- Communism is regarded as a more extreme form of socialism.

TYPES OF COMMUNISM
- Marxism-Leninism—emerging in the 1920s, this form of communism was adopted by the Soviet Union during the rule of Vladimir Lenin. The emphasis is on helping the poor rise. It is currently still the most popular form of communism, even after the fall of the Soviet Union.
- Stalinism—characterized by a totalitarian regime, Stalin's Soviet Union focused on industrialization instead of helping the poor.
- Maoism—instead of placing attention on the working urban class, Mao Zedong placed his focus on the working rural class and attempted to deindustrialize society.

CURRENT COMMUNIST COUNTRIES
- North Korea
- Cuba
- People's Republic of China

WHEN TO BULLSHIT
- When discussing the current states of North Korea and China.
- When organizing a working-class riot.

SOCIALISM
Production and distribution of goods by the government.

WHAT IT IS
- Socialism is primarily an economic theory that advocates for collective or governmental control of the production and distribution of goods.
- There are various forms of socialism.
- Some tolerate capitalism so long as the government remains the most powerful influence on the economy, while others require the complete abolition of private enterprise.

BIRTH OF SOCIALISM
- The rise of socialism as a political ideology occurred between 1815 and 1848, as a response to the French Revolution and the Industrial Revolution.
- The political, social, and economic system that arose from this "dual revolution" altered the European identity from one of community values to one of individualism.
- French socialists, such as Henri de Saint-Simon and Charles Fourier, critiqued the industrial society and promoted a socialist doctrine.

IMPORTANT FIGURES
- Karl Marx (1818–1883):
  - Greatly influenced by French utopian socialists.

- Considered the most influential socialist thinker of the nineteenth century.
- *The Communist Manifesto*—written with Friedrich Engels in 1848, argued that capitalism would inevitably fall victim to an internal struggle that would lead to its destruction. The *Manifesto* outlined a theory of communist revolution led by the proletariat that would destroy bourgeois-capitalist society.
- Considered socialism to be the transitional period between capitalism and communism.
- Vladimir Ilyich Lenin (1870–1924):
  - Leader of the Bolshevik Party in Russia.
  - Led the October Revolution of 1917, a coup d'état that overthrew Russia's provisional government. After three years of civil war, Lenin and the Bolsheviks assumed complete control of the country.
  - First leader to put socialism to the test. Lenin was pragmatic, however, and when his efforts to establish the socialist model faced resistance, he introduced the "new economic policy" that allowed for an element of private enterprise to remain.

WHEN TO BULLSHIT
- When discussing the impact of socialism with someone.
- When trying to distinguish between socialism and communism.

MONARCHY

All hail the king.

WHAT IT IS
- A type of government in which one individual (monarch, king, queen, etc.) possesses all political power, either nominally or absolutely. Hereditary rule is a common characteristic, but elective monarchies also exist.

CURRENT MONARCHS

- There are currently forty-four monarchical nations in the world, sixteen of which consider Queen Elizabeth II their head of state.
- Only Brunei, Oman, Qatar, Saudi Arabia, Swaziland, and Vatican City maintain an absolute monarch in the historical sense.

TYPES OF MONARCHY

- Absolute Monarchy—The monarch possesses absolute control of the state and government, ruling his nation as an autocrat. Absolute monarchies are not always authoritarian.
- Constitutional Monarchy—Sovereignty remains nominally in the hands of the monarch, but rests politically with the people. The monarch's power is limited by the existence of a constitution, and he carries out, for the most part, ceremonial functions. Monarchs in some constitutional monarchies, however, retain certain privileges and powers, such as granting pardons and appointing titles of nobility.
- Elective Monarchy—Though the monarch is originally elected, elective monarchies frequently transform into hereditary monarchies. Three exist today: Malaysia, the United Arab Emirates and the papacy.

RULES OF SUCCESSION

- Varies from country to country.
- Constitutional Monarchy—rule of succession usually set forth in a law passed by a representative body.
- Elective Monarchy—monarchs are elected for life by a political body.
- Hereditary Monarchy—the position of monarch is inherited, typically within a royal family that can trace its origins to a historical dynasty/ bloodline.

WHEN TO BULLSHIT
- When traveling abroad (so you don't sound like the "Dumb American").

ARISTOCRACY

Determining who's the best.

WHAT IT IS

- Though its meaning is vague, an aristocracy is any form of government that is ruled by a group of people who are considered the most able or "the best."
- In Plato's *The Republic*, Plato states Aristotle held aristocracy in high regard and claimed that, unlike oligarchy or democracy, which would focus on wealth, an aristocracy would be a government run by those best suited to govern.

ARISTOCRACY IN HISTORY

- The concept of aristocracy originated in Athens, Greece, with a council of prominent citizens who kept the monarchy in check.
- In the Middle Ages in Europe and medieval Japan, the notion of nobility determined "the best" were not the people most educated or intelligent, but rather, the class of society that had the most land. This was known as nobility and feudalism, and the status was perceived as the best because it was hereditary (though sometimes given).
- Nobility would become one of the chief causes of the French Revolution.

WHEN TO BULLSHIT

- When proving that you're the right guy for the job.

OLIGARCHY

The distinguished few.

WHAT IT IS

- From the Greek *oligarkhia*, meaning government by the few, it is a type of government in which political power rests in the hands of a small group of people, generally those who are distinguished by royalty, wealth, military strength, etc.

EXAMPLES OF OLIGARCHIES
- *Vaishali*, the French First Republic government under the Directory, and the Polish-Lithuanian Commonwealth, Sparta, and South Africa.

CORPORATE OLIGARCHY/CORPORATOCRACY
- A power structure in which small, elite groups of individuals or economic entities work in conjunction or under the control of the oligarchy.

IRON LAW OF OLIGARCHY
- German sociologist Robert Michels argued that any political system will eventually evolve into an oligarchy.
- He believed that the practical demands of politics inevitably caused power to become concentrated in the hands of a small and efficient group of people.
- According to the iron law of oligarchy, modern democracies should be considered oligarchies.

WHEN TO BULLSHIT
- When discussing political systems of the past and present (and future?).

TOTALITARIANISM
Rule by one (and only one—or else).

WHAT IT IS
- Government run by a dictator or party with absolute control over the people and land, with an emphasis on nationalism.
- Often this is accomplished through the use of military and propaganda, and is very oppressive in nature.

TOTALITARIANISM THROUGHOUT HISTORY
- Hitler's Germany—Hitler not only censored media, but created propaganda to promote his Nazi regime and the Holocaust. Those who spoke up against the party were imprisoned or sent to concentration camps.

Hitler's Germany was defined by manipulation and coercion, and the people of the land could do nothing about it.

- Stalin's Soviet Union—Stalin created a new constitution reinforcing his power over the land, and is responsible for killing millions in the Great Purges. He attempted to rid the Soviet Union of anyone who spoke out against him.
- Mussolini's Italy—Mussolini allowed for one party, and one party only: the National Fascist Party. He took control of all aspects of communication, and formed a secret police to control any criticism.

TOTALITARIANISM TODAY

- China—The communist government can conduct surveillance and searches through homes and personal records without any warning. It also attempts to silence nonbelievers in labor camps and constantly violates human rights.
- North Korea—The North Korean government has very tight control over media and communications and access online is extremely limited. There are reports of slave labor, torture, and public executions within prison camps.

WHEN TO BULLSHIT
- When you find yourself in a conversation with a bunch of political blowhards.

THE ELECTORAL COLLEGE
Getting the vote out (so others can vote for you).

WHAT IT IS
- The Electoral College was established during the framing of the Constitution.
- Regarding the presidency, there were conflicting thoughts as to whether the people should have the deciding vote or whether Congress should.
- The Electoral College was a middle ground between the two.

- Each state has a certain number of electors, representative of its population.
- This number is achieved by adding the number of senators from the state and the number of representatives.
- When citizens vote in a presidential election, they are actually voting for electors who represent their state.
- These electors then vote in the presidential election.
- The electors generally vote the way the majority of their state sways, but they don't necessarily have to and sometimes don't.

THE 2000 ELECTION

- In the 2000 election, presidential candidate Al Gore won the popular vote, i.e., the vote of the American people, but George W. Bush won the Electoral College vote, thereby making him the next president of the United States of America.

DO WE NEED IT ANYMORE?

- There is great debate whether we still need the Electoral College.
- In states that always swing a certain way, voters in that state who vote differently will not matter.
- As the 2000 election showed, the winner of the popular vote can lose, making the majority of votes not matter.

WHEN TO BULLSHIT

- When discussing if you should bother voting in the next election.
- When you want to sound like you have a good understanding of politics.

THE CONSTITUTION

Laying down U.S. law since 1787.

WHAT IT IS

- The groundwork for the U.S. government.
- Tells Americans what rights they have as citizens of the country.
- Protects the citizens.

WHAT IT SAYS

- The preamble states our reasons for separating from England during the Revolutionary War.
- Following the preamble are seven articles.
- Among other things, the seven articles establish the three branches of government, allow states to carry out their own laws, and establish that the Constitution can change by adding amendments.
- What follows are a list of amendments.

NOTABLE AMENDMENTS

- First Amendment—freedom of speech, religion, the press, assembly, and the right to petition the government.
- Second Amendment—the right to own guns.
- Sixth Amendment—the right to have a fair and speedy trial.
- Thirteenth Amendment—the abolition of slavery.
- Eighteenth Amendment—illegal to make, sell, or transport alcohol (this came about during Prohibition. Needless to say, it has been repealed).
- Nineteenth Amendment—women's right to vote.

WHEN TO BULLSHIT

- When you need to use one of your rights to bullshit through a situation. (Why do you think lawyers are so good at BS? They know their shit.)

BRANCHES OF GOVERNMENT

It's all about keeping each other in check.

EXECUTIVE

- Composed of the president, the vice president, and the fifteen cabinet members.
- The president can sign legislation into law or veto bills (keep from becoming law).
- If a bill is vetoed, it goes back to Congress. The veto can be overridden with a two-thirds vote from both houses.
- There are only three qualifications for the presidency:

1. A person must be at least thirty-five years old.
2. A person must be a natural-born citizen.
3. A person must have lived in the country for at least fourteen years.

- The vice president resides as president of the Senate, and in the case of a tie, he provides the final vote.

LEGISLATIVE

- Composed of both the House of Representatives and the Senate, elected by the people, and together make up Congress.
- House of Representatives: representation is proportional to the number of people living in the state.
- Senate: each state is represented equally.
- Congress has the power to declare war and pass legislation.

JUDICIAL

- The Supreme Court and the federal courts.
- Members are appointed by the president and have to be confirmed by the Senate.
- Judges appointed to the Supreme Court serve until they die.
- The Supreme Court is the highest court in the nation.

WHEN TO BULLSHIT

- When discussing anything that has to do with American politics and government. Even if you don't know what's going on currently, having a passing grasp and understanding of the system will get you through it.

Chapter 15

Philosophy— A Theory for All Seasons

PRISONER'S DILEMMA

What happens when separated.

WHAT IT IS

- The prisoner's dilemma is a fundamental problem of game theory that deals with issues of cooperation and conflict.
- Originally created by Merrill Flood and Melvin Dresher in 1950 as a part of an investigation into game theory by the Rand Corporation, but was given its name by Albert W. Tucker.
- Example: Tom and Mark are caught robbing an elderly woman at gunpoint. They are brought to jail and placed in separate interrogation rooms. Each is concerned only with his own well-being. Both men are provided with the following information: If you confess, and thereby implicate your partner, and your partner does not confess, you will be let free and you partner will do time. If your partner confesses, and thereby implicates you, and you do not confess, he will be let go and you will do the time. If you both confess, you will both serve time with the option

of early parole. Finally, if neither of you confesses, both of you will be charged only with firearm possession.

DILEMMA
- Though confession is the rational strategy for each individual, the outcome is worse when both confess than it would be if both remained silent.

APPLICATIONS OF THE PRISONER'S DILEMMA
- Economics and business strategy, arms races, climate change.

WHEN TO BULLSHIT
- Use prisoner's dilemma in the workplace to help weigh out your options or to simply screw around with colleagues.

SOCRATES
Learning through questioning.

HIS LIFE
- Socrates lived from 469 to 339 B.C. in Athens, Greece.
- He is one of the founders of Western philosophy, which is still around today.
- Socrates did not leave behind any written work, and all that is known about him comes from Xenophon, a Greek historian of the time, and Plato.
- Plato was Socrates's prize student. He also would become a famous philosopher.
- Socrates was put on trial for his remaining loyalty to Sparta after Sparta had been taken over by Athens. Socrates famously died when the court ordered him to drink the poison hemlock.

THE SOCRATIC METHOD
- Socrates is most known for his implementation of the Socratic Method.
- Instead of a teacher simply giving information to the pupils, the teacher asks the students a series of questions. Through answering the questions,

the students gain a better understanding of not only the subject being taught, but their comprehension of the material.

> **WHEN TO BULLSHIT**
> • Use the Socratic Method to learn more about a favorite bullshitting topic. You'll turn the focus to the other person but come out looking like the expert on the subject.

DAVID HUME
The irrationality of induction.

HIS LIFE
• Hume was a Scottish philosopher who lived from 1711 to 1776.
• He is one of the most prominent figures of Western philosophy and of the Scottish Enlightenment.
• Hume is most recognized for his contributions to philosophical empiricism and skepticism.

MAJOR WORKS
• *A Treatise of Human Nature* (1739–1740)
• *Enquiry Concerning Human Understanding* (1748)
• *Enquiry Concerning the Principles of Morals* (1751)

PROBLEM OF INDUCTION
• Induction is the process by which general conclusions are drawn from specific experiences (e.g., every ice cube I have touched so far has been cold; therefore all ice cubes are cold).
• Hume argues that inductive arguments cannot be rational because they presuppose that the future will resemble the past.
• Justifications for induction fall victim, he explains, to circular reasoning. One cannot claim that, because induction has worked in the past, it will continue to work in the future.
• This type of argument assumes what it is trying to prove—that induction is valid.

- Hume adopts a skeptical solution to the problem of induction. Though we cannot rationally justify induction, we engage in such reasoning as the result of custom or habit, and we benefit from doing so. He explains, "all inferences from experience, therefore, are effects of custom, not of reasoning. Custom, then, is the great guide of human life."

INFORMATION TO USE WHEN BULLSHITTING
- Kant stated that Hume woke him from his "dogmatic slumbers."

WHEN TO BULLSHIT
- When you are stuck in a circular argument. If done right, you'll not only come across as smart and helpful, but you'll also get your way.

RENÉ DESCARTES
Separation of mind and body

HIS LIFE
- Descartes was a French philosopher, physicist, and mathematician who lived from 1596 to 1650.
- He is an important figure in the Scientific Revolution and is widely regarded as the father of modern philosophy.
- He is most famous for his *Meditations on First Philosophy*, in which he aims to provide answers to a wide range of epistemic and metaphysical questions about existence, the senses, and God.
- Descartes is also thought to have provided the first philosophical framework for the natural sciences.

OTHER IMPORTANT WORKS
- *Discourse on the Method* (1637)—Descartes's first published work.
- *Principles of Philosophy* (1644)—Sets forth Descartes's views on the laws of physics, including the belief that a vacuum is impossible.
- *Passions of the Soul* (1649)—Dedicated to Princess Elisabeth of Bohemia. Outlines how the emotional/moral life of a human being is connected to the union of the body and soul.

CARTESIAN DUALISM

- Descartes argued that the mind and body are separate from one another, but work in harmony.
- The mind and body interact, he claimed, via the pineal gland.

INFORMATION TO USE WHEN BULLSHITTING

- Descartes's most famous quote is *cogito ergo sum* (I think, therefore I am).

WHEN TO BULLSHIT

- When trying to sound educated.
- When discussing the connection between your mind and body, though maybe not first thing in the morning.

IMMANUEL KANT

A man looking for reason.

HIS LIFE

- Kant was a German philosopher who lived from 1724 to 1804.
- One of the most important philosophers of the European Enlightenment.

IMPORTANT WORKS

- *Critique of Pure Reason* (1781; second edition, 1787) is considered to be one of the most important works in the history of philosophy.
- It focuses on the question of "what and how much can understanding and reason know apart from all experience?" and aims to reach a decision about whether or not metaphysics in general is possible or impossible.
- Some of his most influential theories are found in *Grounding for the Metaphysic of Morals*.
- Argues that the only principle that is absolutely necessary and can properly command human action is the categorical imperative.
- Provides three principal formulations of the categorical imperative:
  - The first formulation, or the formula of universalizability, states: "Act only according to that maxim whereby you can at the same time will that it should become a universal law."

- The second, the formula of humanity, requires that you: "Act in such a way that you treat humanity, whether in your own person or in the person of another, always at the same time as an end and never simply as a means."
- The third formulate states: "So act as though you were, through your maxims, a law making member of a kingdom of ends."

WHEN TO BULLSHIT
- Use Kant when discussing metaphysics . . . and good luck.

FRIEDRICH NIETZSCHE
A man without a God.

HIS LIFE
- Nietzsche was born in Germany and lived from 1844 to 1900.
- He published his first book, *The Birth of Tragedy*, in 1872.
- Over a period of ten years, Nietzsche would come to write eleven more books.
- In January 1889, Nietzsche suffered from a nervous breakdown (the legend goes he witnessed a man beating his horse, rushed to stop him, and collapsed to the ground).
- After suffering from two strokes in 1898, he remained unable to walk and talk.
- His sister published his writings after his death; however, she edited them to align with Nazi principles, a party Nietzsche himself loathed.

"GOD IS DEAD"
- In one of his most known statements, Nietzsche claims "God is dead," stating new developments in science killed the Christian God.
- As he sees it, the principles from the Christian God no longer serve as the basis of value or principles for people to live by.
- Nietzsche believed this realization would lead to nihilism, the rejection of all religious principles and the notion that life is meaningless.

THE WILL TO POWER
- Considered Nietzsche's most influential work, *The Will to Power* is a collection of his notes published posthumously where he attempts to describe the driving force for man.
- Nietzsche claims that in all aspects of life, people set out to impose their will onto others.

WHEN TO BULLSHIT
- Use Nietzsche when discussing advancements in technology. Nothing perks someone's ears more than saying "God is dead." You'll definitely get his attention.

SØREN KIERKEGAARD
Existential with a twist of religion.

HIS LIFE
- Kierkegaard was a Danish philosopher and religious author who lived from 1813 to 1855.
- Kierkegaard has been referred to as the "Father of Existentialism," even though much of his work involved pursuing a faith in God, something his biggest proponents didn't believe in.

FEAR AND TREMBLING
- One of the vital pieces to the origins of existentialism.
- In trying to understand the anxiety Abraham must have felt when God told him to kill his only son Isaac as an act of faith, Kierkegaard develops two figures: "The Knight of Faith" and "The Tragic Hero."
  - The Tragic Hero—Acts committed by the Tragic Hero are within the ethical, or social codes, and the Tragic Hero acts based on that code. Kierkegaard agues Abraham did not fall under this category.
  - The Knight of Faith—Abraham knows killing his son is wrong, but not doing it would go against God. This turns ethics into temptation. The Knight of Faith shows that faith is grounds for rising above ethics.

THE THREE SPHERES OF EXISTENCE

- Kierkegaard argues there are three levels of existence.
  - The Aesthetic—living to satisfy one's own needs or developing one's own talents.
  - The Ethical—someone who acts for others without thinking of personal gains.
  - The Religious—living only for God.

WHEN TO BULLSHIT

- Use the work of Kierkegaard when discussing religion with someone.
- Use the work of Kierkegaard when discussing existentialism with someone.

JEAN-PAUL SARTRE

Being what the eyes make of you.

HIS LIFE

- Sartre, a French philosopher, playwright, novelist, screenwriter, and political activist, lived from 1905 to 1980.
- Sartre is most known for his work in existentialism and Marxism.
- In 1964, Sartre was awarded the Nobel Prize in Literature but turned it down.

BEING AND NOTHINGNESS

- Sartre's own theory on the consciousness of being.
- Sartre rejects duality and Kant's theory of noumenon, and suggests the only reality is appearance.
- Sartre suggests there are two types of being.
  - In-itself—inanimate objects of the external world that simply exist with no active or passive consciousness.
  - For-itself—something that is conscious of its awareness and has feelings, such as man.
- Sartre claims that a gaze from another person makes a being-for-itself aware of itself and become objectified and alienated. That gaze deprives the existence of a being-for-itself and replaces it with a being-in-itself.

- The awareness of being perceived causes one to deny one's consciousness and the other person's consciousness, and the other person is perceived as being superior.
- To reverse the relationship, a person will attempt to objectify the other person.

WHEN TO BULLSHIT
- Use Sartre as a pickup line in a bar, i.e., You didn't mean to stare at her from across the room, but now that you've deprived her of existence as a being-for-itself, maybe you can make up for it by getting her a drink.

JOHN RAWLS
The veil of fairness.

HIS LIFE
- Rawls was born in Maryland and lived from 1921 to 2002. He taught at Harvard University for forty years.
- Rawls is best known for his contributions to moral and political philosophy, with his most famous work being *A Theory of Justice*.

A THEORY OF JUSTICE
- Rawls makes his own moral theory that he calls "justice as fairness," which presents an alternative to utilitarianism.
- Rawls believes that with utilitarianism some people's rights are sacrificed for the greater good.
- Rawls devised his principles of justice based on what he calls the "original position."
- People have a "veil of ignorance" when deciding principles of justice. Only by making a person unaware of their race, creed, social status, and health, can they decide what's truly just.
- The first principle of justice, which is absolute and cannot be violated, states that every person can have democratic rights such as freedom of speech, assembly, personal property, and the right to vote and run for office.

- The second principle of justice states that social and economic inequalities are justified if they are beneficial to the disadvantaged members of society, and that everyone must have the same opportunity to acquire these positions.

WHEN TO BULLSHIT
- When in the middle of a conversation about justice and politics.

JOHN STUART MILL
A utilitarian with a focus on social reform.

HIS LIFE
- One of the greatest philosophers to come out of Victorian England.
- Greatly influenced by and supportive of utilitarianism, the idea that actions can only be judged as good or bad based on their results, Mill focused his work on social reform, and protecting the rights of the individual.
- Mill focused on the rights of women in particular, and is considered to be one of the first feminists.
- Mill applied his work to political economy, and also was a member of parliament.

ON LIBERTY
- Mill's most well-known work.
- It draws many of its conclusions from utilitarianism.
- Mill states any person should have the liberty to do whatever he wants to do and think whatever he wants to think, as long as it doesn't create harm to anyone else.
- Mill stresses that the individual's happiness is what is most important (as long as they are not harming others).
- He believes that with a majority (such as society or government), morals and standards are set disregarding the individual.
- He argues individual decision making is what's most important and should thus be represented by the government.

WHEN TO BULLSHIT
- When trying to get away with something—because, according to Mill, you should be able to do whatever you want as long as you don't hurt anybody in the process.

MARTIN HEIDEGGER
On being.

HIS LIFE
- Heidegger was born in Germany in 1889 and died in 1976.
- Heidegger's work focuses on existentialism and phenomenology, or the study of consciousness and being, and his book, *Being and Time*, is his most important work.
- Heidegger was a staunch supporter of Adolf Hitler and the Nazi Party; only after denazification, in 1950, was he once again allowed to teach at Freiburg University.
- Heidegger's affiliation with the Nazi Party is still controversial to this day.

BEING AND TIME
- Published in 1927, the book was never fully completed and is one of the most complicated to follow.
- Heidegger states that Western philosophy has ignored the question of what being actually is.
- Heidegger calls the sense of being *dasein*, and argues that ideas that are concrete and specific form the foundation of perception, and thinking abstractly leads to confusion.
- Heidegger states that only when being experienced is time meaningful. Time as a concept on its own is not meaningful.

WHEN TO BULLSHIT
- When you need to explain why you (or "your being") were late for that meeting.

Chapter 16

Sports—
Stats Don't Lie
(People Do)

BASEBALL

America's pastime.

HOW IT STARTED

- The first mention of baseball was in a British publication in 1744.
- In 1845, Andrew Cartwright created the Knickerbocker Rules, a code that detailed how to play baseball.
- Many of these rules are still in place today.

THE WORLD SERIES

- The championship between the two best teams of the season.
- They play best-of-seven.
- The winner of four games wins.
- The New York Yankees have won the World Series more than any other team with twenty-seven wins.

FAMOUS PLAYERS

- Babe Ruth—AKA "The Sultan of Swat." When Babe Ruth retired in 1935, he held the record for most homeruns at 714. His record would not be beaten until 1974 by Hank Aaron.
- Jackie Robinson—First black player to enter the major leagues in 1947 contributing greatly to the end of segregation in baseball.
- Joe DiMaggio—Played all thirteen years of his career with the Yankees and is best known for achieving a fifty-six game hitting streak, a record that still stands today.

TERMS

- Clutch hitter: a high honor for a player, the clutch hitter is able to hit the ball when it matters the most and the game is on the line.
- Golden sombrero: when a player strikes out four times in a game.
- Hit and run: when a runner on first base makes a break for second as the pitch is thrown. If the batter does not hit the ball, the runner will be stealing the base and it will result in an out.
- Runs batted in (RBI): the number of runs scored as a direct result of the person at bat.

WHEN TO BULLSHIT

- When sitting through a baseball game.
- When making conversation with coworkers around the water cooler.
- When trying to fit in at a sports bar.

BASKETBALL

Shooting hoops.

HOW IT STARTED

- In 1891, Dr. James Naismith invented basketball at a YMCA in Springfield, Massachusetts, as a way to keep students occupied during the winter.
- It was called basket ball (then two words) because students would throw a ball into peach baskets.

- Nine of the original thirteen rules have been modified and are still used in basketball today.

THE NATIONAL BASKETBALL ASSOCIATION (NBA)

- In the playoffs, sixteen teams from the Eastern Conference and the Western Conference play against each other in a best-of-seven tournament.
- The final four teams play against each other in the NBA Conference Finals.

FAMOUS PLAYERS

- Larry Bird—player for the Boston Celtics. He was Most Valuable Player (MVP) three times, won the championship three times and an Olympic Gold Medal, and had a rivalry with Magic Johnson that was legendary.
- Michael Jordan—player for the Chicago Bulls. He was MVP seven times and led the Bulls to six championships.
- Wilt Chamberlain—thought by many to be one of the greatest basketball players in history, Chamberlain was MVP four times, and won one championship with the Philadelphia 76ers and one with the Los Angeles Lakers. Before playing in the NBA, Chamberlain played for the Harlem Globetrotters.

INFORMATION TO USE WHEN BULLSHITTING

- Basketball and hockey are the only two major sports in which every team faces off with one another.
- The Boston Celtics have won the most NBA championships.

WHEN TO BULLSHIT

- When attending a basketball game.
- When watching *Space Jam* or *Kazaam* and making conversation (though, any conversation might be better than that—basketball is just one of many options).

FOOTBALL

American football that is . . .

THE HISTORY
- The roots of football trace back to both rugby and soccer.
- In 1876, Walter Camp, considered to be the father of football, created the first rules for American football.
- In the early twentieth century, football spread across college campuses.
- The National Football League (NFL) was established in 1920 (originally, it was called the American Professional Football Association).

COLLEGE FOOTBALL
- National Collegiate Athletics Association (NCAA) divides college football into three divisions: Division I, II, and III.
- Division I is composed of the top athletic teams.
- There are no playoffs in college football and no "champion." Instead teams play Bowl Games among their divisions.
- The Heisman Trophy is given each year to the most outstanding player.

THE NATIONAL FOOTBALL LEAGUE
- Currently, there are thirty-two teams in the NFL.
- The NFL is divided into two conferences: the National Football Conference (NFC) and the American Football Conference (AFC).
- In the playoffs, six teams from each conference play against one another. The two winning teams play against each other in the Super Bowl.
- Three teams have currently won the Super Bowl the most times with five wins: the Pittsburgh Steelers, the San Francisco 49ers, and the Dallas Cowboys.

WHEN TO BULLSHIT
- When watching the Super Bowl.
- When talking about college football—simply bring up the need for playoffs instead of the current Bowl system, and let others take it from there.

HOCKEY
Fighting on the ice for the puck.

THE HISTORY
- Though its origins are unknown, the first game played with established rules was in 1875 in Montreal, Canada, by students of McGill University.
- The National Hockey League (NHL) was established in 1917.
- In 1920, ice hockey was played in the Olympic Summer Games in Belgium for the first time.

THE NATIONAL HOCKEY LEAGUE
- Divided into two conferences: Eastern and Western, which are then divided into three divisions.
- For the most part, teams within the same division and conference faceoff against each other.
- In a regular season, eighty-two games are played and teams are given points:
  - If a team wins, it's two points.
  - If a team ties, it's one point.
  - If a team loses in overtime, it's one point.
  - If a team loses, it's zero points.
- The eight teams from each conference with the most points face off in the playoffs, which is made up of four rounds. The two winners from these rounds face off in the Stanley Cup, which they play best-of-seven.

NOTABLE PLAYERS
- Henrik Sedin, captain for the Vancouver Canucks. In the 2009–2010 season, Sedin won the Hart Trophy and was deemed MVP.
- Sidney Crosby, captain for the Pittsburgh Penguins. In 2009, Crosby became the youngest captain to win the Stanley Cup in NHL history.

INFORMATION TO USE WHEN BULLSHITTING
- The Montreal Canadiens have won more Stanley Cup championships than any other team, with twenty-three wins, and one win before the formation of the NHL.

- Hockey is one of the few sports where violence is encouraged, but penalties are enforced. While checking or smashing into another player is allowed, boarding or smashing the other player into the boards will be penalized.

WHEN TO BULLSHIT
- When watching the Stanley Cup or a hockey game with people who are really into the sport.
- When in the company of Canadians.

SOCCER

Goooooaaaaal!
AKA Football (everywhere but the United States)

THE HISTORY
- In 1848, Cambridge University first attempted to standardize a set of rules for the game of football but no one could fully agree.
- On October 26, 1863, the Football Association formed in London and established the official rules to the game.
- On May 21, 1904, the Fédération Internationale de Football Association (FIFA) was established.
- Soccer became an Olympic sport in 1904.

FIFA WORLD CUP
- The World Cup is a soccer tournament held every four years to determine the championship.
- Brazil has won the most World Cup Championships, with five wins.
- Italy has won the World Cup four times.

PLAYERS TO KNOW
- Pelé is considered one of the greatest players of all time. He played in four World Cup Championships with Brazil, and is the top scorer of all time.

- Diego Maradona is also considered one of the greatest players in soccer, playing in four World Cups for Argentina. He is most known for the "hand of God," from the 1986 World Cup, in which he scored with a handball that wasn't penalized because the referee didn't see it.

WHEN TO BULLSHIT
- When watching the World Cup.
- When abroad in Europe making friends will be *much* easier if you have even the faintest knowledge of the sport.

SWIMMING

The breaststroke, the backstroke, and the bullshit.

THE HISTORY
- Swimming was introduced at the first modern Olympic Games in Athens in 1896.
- Women were first allowed to swim in the Olympics in 1912.
- In 1956, the butterfly stroke became a separate competition. From 1933 until then, it had been used by swimmers in the breaststroke competition.

COMPETITIVE SWIMMING
- There are four strokes in competitive swimming:
  1. Front crawl (AKA freestyle)
  2. Backstroke
  3. Breaststroke
  4. Butterfly
- Medley swimming is when all four strokes are performed.

NOTABLE SWIMMERS
- Michael Phelps—American swimmer who has won sixteen gold medals, broken five records in one meet, and has won more Olympic medals than anyone else in the history of the Olympics.

- Dara Torres—American swimmer who was the first to compete in five Olympic games. In the 2008 Beijing Olympics, Torres competed at the age of forty-one, making her the oldest American swimmer in Olympic history.

INFORMATION TO USE WHEN BULLSHITTING
- In 1984, Olympic swimming had its first tie. U.S. swimmers Carrie Steinseifer and Nancy Hogshead completed the 100-meter freestyle competition touching the wall at a time of 55.92 seconds.

WHEN TO BULLSHIT
- When chatting up the hot lifeguard at the pool.

TENNIS
The BS Open.

THE HISTORY
- Monks in the twelfth century began playing a game very similar to tennis, but used their hands instead of a racket.
- In London, 1874, the rules for a game similar to today's tennis were laid out.
- The first Wimbledon Tournament was held in 1877, and by 1882, the rules for modern tennis were established.

THE TOURNAMENTS
- Tournaments are generally divided by gender, number of players (singles or doubles), and mixed doubles (one male, one female).
- There are four main tournaments, called the "Grand Slam" tournaments:
  1. The Australian Open—played on hard courts
  2. The French Open—played on clay
  3. Wimbledon—played on grass
  4. The US Open—played on hard courts
- Having a Grand Slam means winning all four tournaments in the same year.

NOTABLE PLAYERS

- Serena Williams has won eleven titles from a Grand Slam tournament. Her sister, Venus, has won seven.
- Raphael Nadal has won five Grand Slam singles titles and also took home the gold medal from the 2008 Beijing Olympics.
- Rod Laver won all four Grand Slams twice in his career, one time in 1962, and the other in 1969.

WHEN TO BULLSHIT

- When talking to someone who is really into tennis.
- If you ever bump into Anna Kournikova—hopefully you'll be able to get a few words in between the drooling.

WRESTLING

There's nothing fake about this (except you).

FREESTYLE WRESTLING

- One of the two styles of wrestling featured in the Olympics.
- Wrestlers use their full bodies to get their opponent to the ground in a three-minute period.
- Women's freestyle wrestling was featured in the 2004 Olympics.

GRECO-ROMAN WRESTLING

- The other form of wrestling featured in the Olympics.
- Greco-Roman wrestling is almost identical to freestyle wrestling, only the athletes are not allowed to attack the legs or use their legs as a defense. They must rely entirely on their upper-body strength.
- Modeled after the wrestling style of the ancient Olympians.
- Greco-Roman wrestling does not include women.

WRESTLING TERMINOLOGY

- Breakdown—when a player gets the opponent on the mat, lying on his stomach or side.

- Par terre—when one player is on his hands and knees, taking on a passive role.
- Tie-up—when a player grabs the opponent's upper body while standing. This is used to gain control.

WHEN TO BULLSHIT
- When attending a high school or college wrestling match.
- When arguing the merits of why World Wrestling Entertainment (WWE) is fake.

SCANDALS
Adrenaline run amok.

THE WHITE SOX THROW THE WORLD SERIES
- In 1919, the Chicago White Sox played in the World Series against the Cincinnati Reds.
- The first baseman and six other players teamed up with a group of gamblers and decided to throw the games.
- Shortly upon losing all five games, their plans were discovered and all the players involved were banned from baseball permanently.

PETE ROSE GAMBLES
- Rose was Rookie of the Year in 1963, MVP in 1973, and won three World Series.
- When he was manager of the Cincinnati Reds, reports spread that Rose was gambling on his team.
- In 1987, Rose was banned from baseball.
- In 2007, Pete Rose admitted that he bet on his team "every night."

FIGURE SKATING BECOMES A CONTACT SPORT
- In the 1994 Winter Olympics, figure skater Nancy Kerrigan was leaving a practice when she was approached by a man and hit in the knee with a baton.
- It was later revealed that the man who hit Kerrigan had been hired by the ex-husband of Tonya Harding, a fellow figure skater. Harding

claimed she knew about the attack afterward; however, her ex-husband claimed she knew the whole time.

- After finishing eighth at the Olympics, Harding was stripped of her previous title and banned from figure skating.

PLAYERS JUICE UP

- In 2002, the issue of steroid use in baseball came to a head.
- In 2004, José Canseco released an autobiography claiming that 80 percent of all players used steroids.
- Steroid use had become so bad that Congress stepped in, leading to new testing and disciplines.

WHEN TO BULLSHIT

- If sports are really not your thing and you're with someone who enjoys them, you can always fall back on these topics to get you through.

OLYMPICS

Going for the Gold.

THE HISTORY

- The Olympics were originally held in Olympia, Greece.
- It is uncertain when the first Olympic games were played; however, the earliest record shows they were played in 776 B.C., with only one game: a 192 meter race.

THE OLYMPICS TODAY

- The Olympic Games are held every two years, alternating between the Winter Olympic Games and the Summer Olympic Games (making it every four years for the season not being played).

THE WINTER OLYMPICS

- There are currently fifteen sports played in the Winter Olympic Games, including cross-country skiing, bobsledding, figure skating, ice hockey, and speed skating.

THE SUMMER OLYMPICS
- There are currently twenty-eight sports played in the Summer Olympic Games, including rowing, diving, gymnastics, volleyball, and wrestling.
- Past sports that are no longer played include Polo and Tug-of-War.

GOLD MEDAL WINNERS TO USE IN CONVERSATION
- Mary Lou Retton—The first American woman to win a gold medal in gymnastics in 1984. She would also win the all-around gold medal that year. To this day, she remains the only American to win the title of All-Around Olympian.

INFORMATION TO USE WHEN BULLSHITTING
- Baseball has been removed from the 2012 Olympic Games, and will be replaced with rugby sevens and golf.
- The five major regions of the world are represented by the five Olympic Rings. They are the Americas, Asia, Europe, Oceana, and Africa.

WHEN TO BULLSHIT
- Well, when watching the Olympics. Pretty straightforward, don't you think?

WINTER SPORTS
Breaking the ice.

SKIING
- The oldest skis on record were discovered in Russia and are 8,000 years old.
- In the eighteenth century, Norwegian scouts used skis while spying on enemies and parts of the Swedish Army used skiing for training.
- Today, there are six different types of skiing:
  1. **Cross Country Skiing**—Skiing on flat land.
  2. **Downhill or Alpine Skiing**—Skiing down a mountain.
  3. **Backcountry Skiing**—Skiing in unmarked and ungroomed slopes.
  4. **Freestyle Skiing**—Performing tricks and jumps while skiing.

5. **Telemark Skiing**—Similar to downhill skiing, however the boots are only connected to the skis by the toes, leaving the heels free.
6. **Adaptive Skiing**—Alpine skiing for those with disabilities.

SNOWBOARDING

- The first marketed snowboard appeared in 1965, and was known as Sherman Poppen's Snurfer (snurfer meaning snow surfer). It featured a rope in the front of the board for control and steel tacks to hold the rider's feet.
- Tricks to know:
  1. **Ollie:** The basis for almost all tricks. The tail of the board is used to spring it into the air so one doesn't have to jump.
  2. **Nollie:** Using the nose of the board to spring into the air.
  3. **Frontside:** When the rider's front is facing the outside of a rotation's arc when performing a spin or trick.
  4. **Backside:** When the rider's back is facing the outside of a rotation's arc when performing a spin or trick.
  5. **1080:** When a rider spins three full rotations (1080 degrees).

WHEN TO BULLSHIT
- When making conversation on the ski lift.
- When trying to distract someone so you never go past the bunny slopes.

Chapter 17

Food & Drink—Gourmet in an Instant

BEER
Brew-haha.

HOW IT'S MADE
- The main ingredients in beer are malt, water, yeast, and hops.
- Beer is made in five processes:
  1. Malting: The grains are heated and dried out.
  2. Mashing: The grains steep in hot water, releasing sugar. The water is then drained, leaving a liquid called wort.
  3. Boiling: The wort is boiled and hops are added.
  4. Fermenting: When the wort is cool, it is strained and placed in a sealed container. The fermentation process begins when the yeast is added.
  5. Bottling: The liquid now has alcohol in it, but is not carbonated. It is bottled and can be carbonated artificially or naturally from the carbon dioxide released from the yeast.

INTERESTING FACTS

- The oldest recipe for beer dates back to 2000 B.C. and the Babylonians. They even had a goddess, Ninkasi, dedicated to beer.
- Chicha is an Incan beer made from corn found in Latin America. To ferment the corn quicker, the beer is made with human saliva.

WHEN TO BULLSHIT

- When trying to impress someone at a bar with your knowledge.
- When making small talk at a bar.
- When trying to get a free drink.
- When your inebriated state makes you a little too chatty, at least this BS isn't belligerent.

WINE

Crush it.

ABOUT WINE

- There are six types of wine.
  1. Red wine—made from red grapes
  2. White wine—usually made from white grapes
  3. Rosé or blush wine—made from a red grape, but the skin is taken out during the process leaving a pink color
  4. Sparkling wine—contains carbon dioxide
  5. Dessert wine—sweeter wines
  6. Fortified wine—has spirits such as brandy added to it

WINE AND FOOD PAIRINGS

- White wines—with white meat and fish.
- Red wines—with red meat and sauces.
- Heavy wines (rich in taste)—with heavy dishes, light wines with light dishes.
- Sauvignon/Fumé Blanc—a floral wine best served with grilled white meat.

- Shiraz/Syrah—full and fruity wine, best with meat dishes or roasted chicken.
- Merlot—soft and plum-like, best with a pesto pasta.
- Chardonnay—fruity wine best with grilled fish.
- Chianti/Sangiovese—full and crisp wine, best with meat, pasta, and fowl.
- Zinfandel—fruity and dry, best served with grilled chicken or barbeque beef.

WHEN TO BULLSHIT
- When aiming to impress as you watch *Sideways*.
- When aiming to impress your dinner date (find out what she plans on ordering and based on that, suggest a wine).

LIQUOR

Drink the hard stuff; know the hard facts.

WHAT IT IS
- An alcoholic beverage that is distilled instead of fermented.
- Distillation: Alcoholic distillation is the process of separating alcohol from water, by heating an alcohol/water solution and condensing and collecting the alcohol rich vapors that are released. The starting material for most distillations is usually a weak alcoholic solution (5–7 percent v/v ethanol).

TYPES OF LIQUOR
- Spirits—distilled beverages that do not contain any added sugar and have an alcohol content of at least twenty percent. Examples include absinthe, brandy, gin, grappa, rum, tequila, vodka, and whisky.
- Liqueurs—distilled beverages that contain added sugar and flavorings. Examples include Grand Marnier, Frangelico, and American Schnapps.
- Brandy—a matured, distilled beverage from white wine, usually from Thompson seedless grapes.
- Rum—a matured, distilled beverage from molasses or cane sugar. Rum is matured in wooden barrels for a year or longer.

- Vodka—an immature, distilled beverage from grains that can have an alcohol percentage as high as 72.5 percent. Water is often added to reduce the alcohol percentage to 40 to 50 percent.
- Gin—vodka that is flavored with juniper berries and possibly other herbs such as coriander.
- Whisky—a matured, distilled beverage from grain.

WHEN TO BULLSHIT
- When you're the bartender at a party.
- When someone has a question about a certain liquor, you're their guy (especially if they need help *drinking* a certain liquor as well).

STEAK
It's rare to eat something so prime.

FACTOR IN CHOOSING A DELICIOUS STEAK: MARBLING
- White parts of fat found within the steak.
- These enhance flavor and its tenderness.

FACTOR IN CHOOSING A DELICIOUS STEAK: AGING
- Storing the steak to improve its taste.
- Dry aging—placing the carcass in a refrigerated room for twenty-one to twenty-eight days.
- Wet aging—placing the meat in vacuum bags at a temperature of 32° to 34°F.

FACTOR IN CHOOSING A DELICIOUS STEAK: USDA GRADES OF BEEF
- Prime—the best grade of beef with the right amount of aging and a large amount of marbling.
- Choice—less marbling than prime and a little firmer in texture.
- Select—less marbling than choice, and firmer in texture. When cooked, select dries out more easily. Select is the most common grade purchased.

KOBE BEEF
- Japanese steak that costs over $100 per pound.
- The meat is very tender and has a lot of marbling.

TIPS FOR COOKING STEAK
- When cooking cheaper meat, braise or stew the meat.
- If you want your steak rare, it should have an internal temperature of 120°–130°F.
- If you want your steak medium, it should have an internal temperature of 140°–150°F.
- If you want your steak well-done, it should have an internal temperature of 165°–175°F.

WHEN TO BULLSHIT
- When you want to impress at a barbeque.
- When you want to haggle your local butcher.
- When you want to sound like you know exactly what you want at a restaurant.

SEAFOOD
Make sure nothing seems fishy.

TIPS FOR BUYING A WHOLE FISH
- Look at the eyes—bright and clear means it's fresh.
- Dull or gray eyes—may be okay to eat but it will not be fresh.
- Smell the fish.
- If a fish is fresh, it should either smell like clean water or slightly salty. Some fish will even smell like cucumber or melon.
- Do not buy a bad-smelling fish; it will not taste good even after being cooked.
- Check the gills. A fresh fish's gills will be a rich red. If the color is faded, the fish is not fresh.

TIPS FOR BUYING A FILET

- Smell the filet.
- Like the whole fish, when purchasing a filet there should be no sign of bad odors.
- If there is liquid on the meat, it should be clear.
- A milky liquid means the fish is beginning to rot.

SEAFOOD THAT IS BETTER TO BUY FROZEN

- Scallops
- Shrimp
- Octopus or Squid

INFORMATION TO USE WHEN BULLSHITTING

- Flash-frozen fish are just as good (and sometimes better) than fresh fish because they are frozen immediately after being taken on the boat.
- To know if a fish has been flash frozen, make sure the package is vacuum sealed or the fish has a thick cover of ice over it.

WHEN TO BULLSHIT

- When making dinner for your date.
- When trying to look like a good cook.

SPICES

Add a little zest to your BS.

WHAT IT IS

- Spices, including herbs, are dried parts of the plant. These include the seeds, the fruit, the leaves, and even the bark.

PURCHASING SPICES

- To ensure full flavor, it's best to buy the whole spice and then grind it yourself.
- Whole spices will stay fresher for a longer amount of time.

HELPFUL TIPS ABOUT SPICE

- Kosher salt draws out the maximum flavor of all the other spices in a dish, even in chocolate.
- Curry powder contains more than twelve spices in it.
- You can use arrowroot, a thickener, as a substitute for cornstarch.
- Spices have been used for centuries for medicinal purposes.
- Three thousand years ago in Egypt, spices were used for culinary and cosmetic purposes.
- Even today, spices are used in deodorants and perfumes.
- Allspice is a dried berry that has flavors resembling a blend of nutmeg, cinnamon, and cloves.

SPICES YOU SHOULD ALWAYS HAVE

- Salt and pepper—to add flavor to practically anything.
- Cinnamon—for desserts and even chili.
- Chili powder—adds a kick to food, particularly Mexican and Korean food.
- Thyme—good with soups, meat, poultry, and French food.
- Rosemary—good with meat and poultry.
- Basil—used in pesto and good for stews and slow-cooked dishes.
- Oregano—good for pasta, fish, and Italian meals.
- Cumin—good for Mexican and Indian dishes.

WHEN TO BULLSHIT

- When preparing a meal and dessert for someone.
- When trying to impress someone as you shop at the grocery store.
- When someone has cooked for you by correctly identifying a spice.

CHEESE

Know your stuff without seeming cheesy.

WHAT IT IS

- Cheese is the curd of milk separated from the whey and prepared as a food. It consists of the fat and protein from the milk of cows, goats, buffalo, and sheep.

THE HISTORY

- Though there is no conclusive evidence as to exactly when and where cheese originated, it is known that cheese was part of the Sumerian diet as early as 4,000 years before the birth of Christ.
- Most scholars agree that cheese making was brought from Asia Minor to Europe, where Romans developed the art as we know it today.
- From the decline of the Roman Empire until the discovery of America, European monks were considered to be the innovators in cheese making.

TYPES OF CHEESE: GOAT CHEESE

- Cheese made from goat's milk.
- It is most often soft, smooth, and easy to spread.
- Goat cheese is considered to be a healthier cheese because it has a lower fat content, fewer calories, and is more easily digested than other cheeses.
- The taste of goat cheese is greatly influenced by the typical goat diet of bitter plants.

TYPES OF CHEESE: CHEDDAR

- Cheddar cheese originates from an English village of the same name.
- Cheddar is a firm cheese from cow's milk and is one of the most popular, readily available types of cheese.
- The taste depends on the aging process and varies widely, from mild to extra sharp.

TYPES OF CHEESE: BLUE CHEESE

- A common type of cow's or goat's milk that contains blue or green mold.
- Blue cheese was originally produced in caves, where mold was naturally present.
- Today, the mold is either injected into or mixed in with the curds.
- The longer the cheese ages, the more intense its flavor and the smoother its texture becomes.

WHEN TO BULLSHIT

- When preparing appetizers for a party.
- When you want to turn "who cut the cheese" into a good thing.

JUNK FOOD
The calories are empty, but the conversation won't be.

TWINKIES
- In 1930, James A. Dewar, a manager of a baking plant in Chicago, noticed the shortcake pans were not being used because the strawberry season was over. He baked little cakes in them, injecting each one with a banana-cream filling. He named his creation Twinkies.
- During World War II, bananas had to be rationed, and Dewar replaced the banana filling with a vanilla-cream filling.

POTATO CHIPS
- In 1853, Native American George Crum worked as a chef at a resort in Saratoga Springs, New York. One day a diner complained that his French-fried potatoes were cut too thick, and refused to eat them. Crum decided he would rile the diner by making potatoes that were too crispy and thin to eat with a fork. His plan didn't go as planned, and the guest loved the new creation.

M&MS
- Forrest Mars created M&Ms during the Spanish Civil War.
- He noticed soldiers eating chocolate with a sugar coating that prevented the chocolate from melting.
- In 1941, the first M&Ms were sold in cardboard tubes.

INFORMATION TO USE WHEN BULLSHITTING
- In 1979, Daniel White claimed he murdered Harvey Milk and Mayor George Moscone because of a chemical imbalance from eating too much junk food, including candy, cupcakes, and Twinkies. This would become known as the "Twinkie Defense." White was convicted, and in 1981, the "Twinkie Defense" was outlawed.
- July 21 is National Junk Food Day.

WHEN TO BULLSHIT
- When you want to turn junk food into brain food.

HEALTHY FOOD

Make it seem organic.

ORGANIC
- Organic fruits and vegetables are grown without the use of pesticides or synthetic fertilizers, instead using natural fertilizers.
- Organic foods have been shown to have more vitamin C, calcium, phosphorous, magnesium, and iron, and have proven to be rich in antioxidants and phenolic compounds.

BLUEBERRIES
- Blueberries contain more antioxidants than any other fresh fruit, and can lower cholesterol, improve one's vision, prevent and cure urinary tract infections, and even slow down the aging process.

BROCCOLI
- Broccoli contains vitamin C, vitamin A, calcium, fiber, and folic acid.
- Broccoli also contains strong anti-carcinogens which have proven to be wonder drugs for different types of cancers including lung cancer, breast cancer, uterine cancer, and cancer of the intestines.

GREEN TEA
- Green tea is high in EGCG, an antioxidant which inhibits the growth of cancer cells and the formation of blood clots, kills cancer cells without causing harm to healthy tissue, and has shown to lower LDL cholesterol levels.

SALMON
- Salmon contains omega-3 fatty acids, essential fatty acids humans can't make.
- Salmon is high in protein, low in fat, and contains vitamin B12, vitamin B6, niacin, phosphorous, and magnesium.

WALNUTS
- Walnuts are rich in vitamin E, magnesium, fiber, B vitamins, and omega-3 fatty acids.
- Walnuts have more omega-3 fatty acids than any other nut, and incorporating them into your diet reduces the risk of heart disease.

ADDITIONAL INFORMATION TO USE WHEN BULLSHITTING

- Because coconut water is sterile and contains the perfect pH level, it can actually be substituted for blood plasma.
- The sugar in an apple will keep you awake more than the caffeine in coffee.

WHEN TO BULLSHIT

- When convincing someone you're eating healthy (especially when you're not).

DESSERT

Sweet talk 'em.

PIE

- Pies were originally made only with meat and poultry.
- At one point, it was illegal in Kansas to serve ice cream on cherry pie.
- In 1644, Oliver Cromwell declared eating pie to be a pagan activity, and banned pie. The ban was lifted sixteen years later.

CAKE

- The baked Alaska is also known as the Norwegian Omelet. Earlier versions of the dessert had pie crust instead of meringue.
- When Queen Elizabeth II married Prince Philip in 1947, their wedding cake weighed 500 pounds.

CUPCAKES

- In Great Britain, cupcakes are called "fairy cakes."
- People say that cupcakes got their name because in order to bake them, one measured in terms of volume (cups) instead of in terms of weight like you would a cake.

WHEN TO BULLSHIT

- When you don't want the last dish of the night to turn into the last conversation.

B.A. in BS

Upon successful completion of the course of study,

The Bullshit Artist hereby confers upon

_____

the Degree of

Bachelor of Arts

in

Bullshitting

Paul Kleinman

SOURCES

Religion

www.religioustolerance.org
www.bcbsr.com/survey/jmrcls.html
www.cair.com/AboutIslam/IslamBasics.aspx
www.sikhs.org/summary.htm
www.bbc.co.uk/religion/religions/jainism/ataglance/glance.shtml
www.religionfacts.com/scientology/beliefs.htm

Art

www.greeklandscapes.com/greece/athens_museum_archaic.html
www.huntfor.com/
http://heritage-key.com/rome/child-rome-birth-byzantine-empire
www.ehow.com/list_6577211_early-renaissance-art-characteristics.html
www.visual-arts-cork.com/
www.maybenow.com/Compare-Michelangelos-David-1501-1504-Donatellos-David-1428-
     1432-and-Berninis-David-1623-q14504678
www.artchive.com/artchive/baroque.html
www.artinthepicture.com/styles/Expressionism/
www.cubism-asada.com/what_cubism.html
http://arthistory.about.com/cs/arthistory10one/a/dada.htm
www.surrealism.org/
www.arthistoryarchive.com/arthistory/popart/
www.arthistoryarchive.com/arthistory/popart/Neo-Pop-Art.html
www.stuckism.com/info.html
www.artcyclopedia.com/artists/close_chuck.html
www.toyism.com/home/about-us

Film

http://news.bbc.co.uk/2/hi/country_profiles/1131421.stm

www.essortment.com/all/hollywoodgold_rfsl.htm

The New Hollywood: from Bonnie and Clyde to Star Wars, by Peter Kramer. Wallflower Press, 2005.

www.oscars.org

www.filmsite.org/90sintro6.html

www.suite101.com/content/miramax-and-the-evolution-of-independent-cinema-a237844

www.mpaa.org/ratings/what-each-rating-means

www.filmcontact.com/united-states/avatar-introduces-new-technologies-3d-production

www.moviemaker.com/education/page2/film_school_film_education_roundtable_20100121/

Television

http://electronics.howstuffworks.com/tv3.htm

www.plasmatvscience.org/theinnerworkings.html

www.practical-home-theater-guide.com/lcd-display.html

www.museum.tv/eotvsection.php?entrycode=goldenage

www.ehow.com/list_6053465_effects-dvr-advertising.html

http://electronics.howstuffworks.com/sitcom3.htm

www.museum.tv/eotvsection.php?entrycode=soapopera

http://reality-tv.lovetoknow.com/History_of_Reality_Television

www.nyu.edu/classes/stephens/History%20of%20Television%20page.htm

http://ezinearticles.com/?Fox-Network-Tclovicion-History&id=1465703

www.thehistoryof.net/history-of-cable-tv.html

www.fcc.gov/cgb/kidszone/history_cable.html

http://en.wikipedia.org/wiki/Broadcast_programming

Books

www.mysterynet.com/timeline/history-of-mystery/

www.topmystery.com/authors/biography/Jim-Thompson

www.mania.com/top-20-greatest-horror-writers-alltime_article_113153.html

http://en.wikipedia.org/wiki/H._P._Lovecraft

www.horror.org

www.raybradbury.com/books/fahrenheit451.html

www.cliffsnotes.com/study_guide/literature/The-Education-of-Henry-Adams-Summary-Analy-sis-and-Original-Text-Chapter-I-Quincy-.id-94,pageNum-10.html

www.sparknotes.com/lit/incoldblood/context.html

www.goodreads.com/shelf/show/historical-fiction

www.wksu.org/features/harveypekar/
www.sparknotes.com/
www.associatedcontent.com/article/2318742/analysis_of_phenomenal_woman_by_maya.html
www.suite101.com/content/robert-frost-s-tricky-poem-a8712
www.helium.com/items/1291525-ee-cummings
www.goodcooking.com/ckbookrv/summer_02/jul_child/master_rev.htm
www.thejoykitchen.com/about.lasso?menu=two
http://astore.amazon.com/httpwwwgetcoo-20/detail/1580081304
www.goodcooking.com/ckbookrv/summer_02/jul_child/master_rev.htm
www.thejoykitchen.com/about.lasso?menu=two
http://astore.amazon.com/httpwwwgetcoo-20/detail/1580081304

Economics

www.investopedia.com
http://economics.about.com/cs/studentresources/f/microeconomics.htm
www.forbes.com/2009/10/04/economics-microeconomics-paul-krugman-opinions-contribu-
    tors-banking.html
www.netmba.com/econ/micro/supply-demand/
http://ingrimayne.com/econ/DemandSupply/OverviewSD.html
www.auburn.edu/~johnspm/gloss/specialization
www.ehow.com/about_5348857_meaning-specialization-economics.html
http://financeworldonline.net/stock-market-basics-101-for-beginners/
http://news.morningstar.com/classroom2/course.asp?docId=145666&page=3&CN=COM
www.moneyinstructor.com/art/bullbearmarket.asp
www.econlib.org/library/Enc1/Reaganomics.html
www.gvsu.edu/hauenstein/index.cfm?id=602EE20B-05B8-8A4D-90F298E71E800588
www.investopedia.com/articles/05/011805.asp
www.investopedia.com/articles/financial-theory/08/game-theory-basics.asp
www.suite101.com/content/the-nash-equilibrium-a65302
www.econlib.org/library/Enc/Marxism.html
www.allaboutworldview.org/marxist-economics.htm
www.businessdictionary.com/definition/laissez-faire-economics.html
www.linfo.org/natural_monopoly.html

Science

http://wiki.answers.com/Q/What_is_the_law_of_independent_assortment
http://biology.about.com/od/mendeliangenetics/ss/lawofsegregation_2.htm
www.spaceandmotion.com/Charles-Darwin-Theory-Evolution.htm

http://mimblewimble.glogster.com/Chemistry-Fun-Facts/
http://simple.wikipedia.org/wiki/String_theory
www.physicspost.com/articles.php?articleId=25&page=2
http://physics.about.com/od/quantumphysics/f/stringtheory.htm
www.space.com/scienceastronomy/090504-mm-supernova.html
http://science.howstuffworks.com/dictionary/astronomy-terms/dark-matter.htm
www.metrofieldguide.com/?p=289
http://hubpages.com/hub/Ecology-Basics
www.novelguide.com/a/discover/ansc_01/ansc_01_00046.html
www.metrofieldguide.com/?p=289
www.differencebetween.net/science/nature/
    difference-between-igneous-sedimentary-and-metamorphic-rocks/
http://geology.about.com/od/nutshells/u/pathbasics.htm#s4
www.qvctc.commnet.edu/brian/cultant.html
www.aaanet.org/about/whatisanthropology.cfm
www.ucmp.berkeley.edu/paleo/paleowhat.html
www.wisegeek.com/what-is-paleontology.htm
http://archaeology.about.com/od/pterms/g/paleontology.htm
www.physorg.com/news9211.html
www.mnsu.edu/emuseum/biology/humanevolution/fosrec.html
www.guardian.co.uk/science/2010/may/06/neanderthals-dna-humans-genome

History

www.king-tut.org.uk/ancient-egypt-history/
http://ehistory.osu.edu/ancient/egypt/overview.cfm
http://rome.mrdonn.org/romulusandremus.html
www.metmuseum.org/toah/hd/roem/hd_roem.htm
www.flowofhistory.com/units/west/11/FC78
www.buzzle.com/articles/renaissance-inventions.html
www.britannica.com/EBchecked/topic/587409/Tennis-Court-Oath
www.sparknotes.com/history/european/frenchrev/summary.html
www.docstoc.com/docs/5955054/things-that-led-to-the-revolutionary-war
www.historycentral.com/revolt/battles.html
http://library.thinkquest.org/05aug/01419/cottongintext.html
www.enotes.com/industrial-revolution-about/introduction
www.u-s-history.com/pages/h283.html
www.civilwar.com
www.civil-war.net

www.historyplace.com/civilwar/
http://history1900s.about.com/od/1930s/p/greatdepression.htm
www.historyonthenet.com/WW1/causes.htm
www.thecorner.org/hist/wwi/index.htm
www.firstworldwar.com/timeline/index.htm
http://europeanhistory.about.com/od/worldwar1/a/ww1stimeline1.htm
www.sparknotes.com/history/european/ww2/summary.html
www.history.navy.mil/photos/events/wwii-eur/normandy/normandy.htm
http://americanhistory.about.com/od/worldwarii/a/wwiioverview_3.htm
www.watson.org/~lisa/blackhistory/civilrights-55-65/
http://americanhistory.si.edu/subs/history/timeline/end/index.html
http://library.thinkquest.org/07aug/00861/thespacerace.htm
http://thinkprogress.org/iraq-timeline/
http://uspolitics.about.com/od/wariniraq/i/iraq_overview_2.htm
http://en.wikipedia.org/wiki/War_in_Afghanistan_(2001–present)

Politics

www.america.gov/st/democracyhr-english/2008/May/20080609194207eaifas0.8688013.html
www.allaboutphilosophy.org/communism.htm
www.fact-index.com/m/ma/maoism.html
www.bbc.co.uk/history/historic_figures/lenin_vladimir.shtml
www.historyguide.org/europe/lenin.html
www.encyclopedia.com/topic/socialism.aspx#3
www.encyclopedia.com/topic/socialism.aspx#1
www.sparknotes.com/philosophy/politics/terms.html
www.wsu.edu/~dee/GLOSSARY/ARISTOC.HTM
www.dictionary.reference.com/browse/oligarchy
www.newworldencyclopedia.org/entry/Oligarchy
www.schoolshistory.org.uk/nazidictatorship.htm
http://library.thinkquest.org/C0112205/stalinsrussia.html
www.areallygoodread.com/Politics-and-Law/Mousollini-the-Totalitarian.aspx
www.naturalnews.com/000851.html
www.cnn.com/SPECIALS/1999/china.50/red.giant/prisons/wu.essay/
http://news.bbc.co.uk/2/hi/country_profiles/1131421.stm
history.howstuffworks.com/american-history/electoral-college1.htm
www.whitehouse.gov/our-government

Philosophy

www.econlib.org/library/Enc/PrisonersDilemma.html

http://plato.stanford.edu/entries/prisoner-dilemma/

www.econlib.org/library/Enc/GameTheory.html

www.philosophypages.com/ph/socr.htm

www.2020site.org/socrates/

http://plato.stanford.edu/entries/hume/

http://en.wikipedia.org/wiki/Problem_of_induction

http://en.wikipedia.org/wiki/David_Hume

http://plato.stanford.edu/entries/descartes/

http://plato.stanford.edu/entries/kant-moral/

www.rep.routledge.com/article/DB047SECT10

http://plato.stanford.edu/entries/kant/

www.infidels.org/library/modern/travis_denneson/power.html

www.egs.edu/library/friedrich-nietzsche/biography/

www.sparknotes.com/philosophy/nietzsche/themes.html

www.suite101.com/content/kierkegaards-three-spheres-of-existence-a221872

www.sparknotes.com/philosophy/sartre/section2.rhtml

www.iep.utm.edu/sartre-ex/

www.wordiq.com/definition/A_Theory_of_Justice

http://plato.stanford.edu/entries/mill/

www.sparknotes.com/philosophy/mill/section3.rhtml

www.dividingline.com/private/Philosophy/Philosophers/Heid/Review_BeingandTimeATranslation-ofSeinandZeit_Heidegger.shtml

Sports

http://en.wikipedia.org/wiki/Baseball

www.nocryinginbaseball.com/glossary/glossary.html

www.askmen.com/top_10/entertainment_60/96d_top_10_list.html

http://inventors.about.com/library/inventors/blbasketball.htm

www.nba.com/history/

www.nfl.com/history

www.ehow.com/how-to_4845444_3_learn-basics-hockey.html

http://sports.espn.go.com/nhl/playoffs/2009/news?columnist=burnside_scott&id=4255637

www.associatedcontent.com/article/5519736/henrik_sedin_mvp.html?cat=14

http://abhisays.com/gaming/maradonas-hand-of-god-goal.html

www.olympic.org

http://swimming.about.com/od/swimmingolympics/tp/Olympic-Swimming-Great-Moments.htm

www.ehow.com/facts_4869431_facts-competitive-swimming.html
www.athleticscholarships.net/history-of-tennis.htm
www.answers.com
http://blackmagic.com/ses/wrest/reference/fsrulesnew.html
www.suite101.com/content/grecoroman-and-freestyle-wrestling-a140528
www.sportspectator.com/fancentral/wrestling/guide05.html
www.findingdulcinea.com/news/sports/2009/feb/11-Biggest-Sports-Scandals.html
www.cardozaplayer.com/article_details.php?contentType=4&typeSub=8
www.infobarrel.com/Michael_Phelps_Olympic_History
http://teacher.scholastic.com/activities/athens_games/history.htm
www.zum.de/whkmla/sp/1011/amazon/amazon1.html
http://skiing.about.com/od/beginningskiers/a/skiingstyles.htm
www.abc-of-snowboarding.com/snowboardinghistory.asp
http://snowboarding.about.com/od/snowboardingtricks/Snowboarding_Tricks.htm

Food/Drink

www.wisegeek.com/how-is-beer-made.htm
www.weirdworm.com/10-weird-beer-facts/
www.winewebcentral.com/winepairing/
www.winegeeks.com/articles/18
www.hyfoma.com/en/content/food-branches-processing-
www.liquorpedia.com/
www.drunkmansguide.com/articles/liquor_styles.php
www.goodcooking.com/steak/steak.htm
www.bigoven.com/glossary/steak
http://fishcooking.about.com/od/howtochoosefreshfish/bb/buyingfish.htm
www.simplebites.net/spices-101-what-you-need-to-know-about-buying-spices/
www.suite101.com/content/a-short-history-of-spices-a91520
www.articlesbase.com/nutrition-articles/spices-every-cook-must-have-in-their-kitchen-from-
the-start-375540.html
http://dictionary.reference.com/browse/cheesewww.godecookery.com/how2cook/cheesnet.htm
www.thenibble.com/reviews/Main/cheese/cheese2/history.asp
www.typesofcheese.com/popular.php
www.punchbowl.com/holidays/national-junk-food-day
www.nytimes.com/2010/08/08/weekinreview/08manny.html?_r=1
www.kitchenproject.com/history/AmericanHeritageRecipes/PotatoChip.htm
http://inventors.about.com/od/mstartinventors/a/ForrestMars.htm

www.associatedcontent.com/article/917301/interesting_facts_about_fruits_nuts_pg2.
   html?cat=22

http://chinesefood.about.com/library/weekly/aa011400a.htm

www.organicfacts.net/health-benefits/vegetable/health-benefits-of-broccoli.html

www.whfoods.com/genpage.php?tname=foodspice&dbid=104

www.suite101.com/content/health-benefits-of-organic-food-a249851

www.healthcastle.com/walnuts-benefits-heart.shtml

http://naturalhealthezine.com/blueberries-health-benefits/

www.foodreference.com/html/fpie.html

www.100cafestreet.com/pie-fun-facts/

www.suite101.com/content/a-brief-history-of-the-humble-cupcake-a151806

http://blogs.smithsonianmag.com/food/2009/07/13/the-strange-history-of-the-wedding-cake/

Index

About the Author

It only seems fitting that Paul Kleinman's first foray into literature be on bullshit. As an art student at the University of Wisconsin, Paul had plenty of time to hone and perfect his bullshitting abilities and has since become a true master. While he eagerly awaits his next opportunity to use these skills, he dreads the next time he will have to write a biographical blurb about himself for fear that he leads a painfully boring and unoriginal life. Paul lives in Boston with his girlfriend and his neuroses.

DAILY BENDER

Want Some More?

Hit up our humor blog, The Daily Bender, to get your fill of all things funny—be it subversive, odd, offbeat, or just plain mean. The Bender editors are there to get you through the day and on your way to happy hour. Whether we're linking to the latest video that made us laugh or calling out (or bullshit on) whatever's happening, we've got what you need for a good laugh.

If you like our book, you'll love our blog. (And if you hated it, "man up" and tell us why.) Visit The Daily Bender for a shot of humor that'll serve you until the bartender can.

Sign up for our newsletter at
www.adamsmedia.com/blog/humor
and download our Top Ten Maxims No Man Should Live Without.